Welcoming the New Millennium

Wisdom from Pope John Paul II

Patricia Mitchell, General Editor

theWORD among us

The Word Among Us Press
9639 Doctor Perry Road
Ijamsville, Maryland 21754
ISBN: 0-932085-31-8

www.wau.org

Design by David Crosson
Copy Editor: Laura Jones

Library of Congress Cataloging-in-Publication Data

John Paul 11, Pope, 1920-
    [Selections. 1999]
    Welcoming the new millennium : wisdom from Pope John Paul II/
Patricia Mitchell, general editor.
        p.   cm.
   ISBN 0-932085-21-0 (pbk. : alk. paper)
   1. Christian life—Catholic authors.   I. Mitchell,
   Patricia, 1953-   II. Title
  BX1378.5.J656A25 1999
  282—dc21

                      99-40926
                      CIP

Made and printed in the United States of America

Table of Contents

Introduction

Pope John Paul II is a man for our times. While others have envisioned dire consequences as the world passes into a new millennium, the Holy Father has predicted a "springtime for Christianity." His entire pontificate has been directed toward preparing Christians everywhere to welcome the third millennium, which he sees as a time of special grace and favor from the Lord.

Given the horrors of the past century, some might think the Pope lives in another world. Yet he is above all a realist. A reading of his encyclicals and letters shows that he is only too aware of the modern-day trends that tend to alienate men and women from each other and from God. He offers a true alternative to the secular "wisdom" of the world—one based on the saving grace and truth of Jesus Christ. This gospel-infused message permeates all of the Holy Father's writing. Like a true believer, Pope John Paul can see the suffering and evil in the world and still not lose hope. After all, Christ has died, is risen, and lives among us!

If some believe that religion is other-worldly and escapist, Pope John Paul II has proven otherwise. Much of his writing concerns itself with promoting the kingdom of God on earth. From human rights to the sanctity of life, from economic justice to marriage and family—all have been on the mind and heart of this Pope. "At stake is the dignity of the human person, whose defense and promotion have been entrusted to us by the Creator" (*On Social Concern*, 47). This concept has been the centerpiece of the Pope's vision for a society in which the human person is valued simply because he is created by God and made in his image and likeness.

Pope John Paul II has guided the Catholic Church to the end of the second millennium using the inspirations of the Second Vatican Council as his road map. Fully involved in writing many of the Vatican II documents when he was a Polish bishop, John Paul II has called Vatican II the "advent" that prepared the church to meet the new millennium. His papal writings constantly refer to the Vatican II documents, and he has continued to develop the critical themes of that Council—from ecumenism to participation of the laity in the life of the church.

Welcoming the New Millennium, Wisdom from Pope John Paul II, is meant to give readers a sampling of the Holy Father's gospel-based vision for our world—and for our own lives. It is a life rooted in Christ, animated by the Holy Spirit, and nourished through the Church and the sacraments. It is a heroic life full of sacrifices for the love of God and others. It is a life worthy of men and women created in the image and likeness of God.

The selections in this book were taken from encyclicals, apostolic letters and exhortations written by John Paul II over the span of his more than twenty years as pontiff, as well as from his speeches and addresses. These writings have been grouped into nine chapters that reflect many of the themes emphasized by the Holy Father over these years. A short biography of John Paul II's life has also been included. The editors at *The Word Among Us Press* have taken the liberty of selecting titles and subtitles to help guide readers through each passage. It is our hope that this book will generate the same energy and excitement that Pope John Paul II generates everywhere he goes. May it inspire Christians to love and serve the Lord with fervor and zeal, and to bring about his kingdom on earth.

Patricia Mitchell
General Editor
The Word Among Us Press

1

Be Not Afraid!

THE COURAGEOUS LIFE OF POPE JOHN PAUL II

By Ellen Wilson Fielding

"The outbreak of the war took me away from my studies and from the university. In that period I also lost my father. . . . At the same time a light was beginning to shine ever more brightly in the back of my mind: the Lord wants me to become a priest. *One day I saw this with great clarity; it was like an interior illumination which brought with it the joy and certainty of a new vocation."*

These words from Pope John Paul II's memoir *Gift and Mystery* (p. 35) describe an extraordinary reaction to a young life drenched in loss. Though he came of age in one of the most hellish times and locations of the twentieth century, John Paul II was able to greet the Catholic world in 1978 as the newly chosen pope with the words, "Be not afraid!" Almost two decades after taking on the Church's difficult final decades of this century, he was able to title one of his books

Crossing the Threshold of Hope. John Paul's balance, sanity, and serenity through the many upheavals of his own life—and the lives of his fellow Christians—are an enduring witness to the abundant grace of God.

Early Losses

Karol Wotyla was born on May 18, 1920, when Poland had re-emerged as an independent country after World War I. His hometown was Wadowice, outside of Krakow. His father, a retired military man, was devoted to God and his family. That family suffered a series of losses that began shortly before Karol's First Communion, when his mother and her newborn baby both died. A few years later, Karol's older brother, who was studying medicine, also became ill and died in December of 1932.

The two survivors—Karol and his father—drew even closer to one another and to God. "Sometimes I would wake up during the night," John Paul recalls, "and find my father on his knees, just as I would always see him kneeling in the parish church. We never spoke about a vocation to the priesthood, but *his example was in a way my first seminary, a kind of domestic seminary*" (*Gift and Mystery*, p. 20).

After Karol finished high school, he and his father moved to Krakow, where he was to study at the Jagiellonion University. His interests and ambitions at this time, despite his strong religious sense, were mainly literary and theatrical. He thought seriously of becoming an actor and a playwright, and planned to study Polish literature.

Meanwhile, Hitler was invading the Sudetenland and annexing Austria. In September of 1939, Poland's turn came. Karol was nineteen years old, just beginning his second year of university studies in Polish literature and discovering the philosophical tug of linguistics—the study of how language works. Within weeks of the new university term, his professors were carted off to labor camps, and Karol went to work in a stone quarry to avoid being deported by the Nazis to a German work camp.

A Dark Time

During this dark time for Poland, Karol became involved in an underground acting group, the *Theater of the Living Word*, led by Mieczyslaw Kotlarczyk. This group produced Polish plays—forbidden by the Nazis—in people's homes, relying almost entirely on the actors' words and delivery to carry the message and keep alive the promise of Polish culture and freedom. For a time Karol lived in the same house as Kotlarczyk and his wife Sofia, and they and their friends would talk about books, plays, Polish culture, and Poland's fate.

It was also at this time that Karol was invited to join a clandestine prayer group organized by a tailor/mystic named Jan Tyranowski. Through Jan, Karol was introduced to Carmelite spirituality and developed a love for the writings of the Spanish mystic St. John of the Cross. John Paul wrote that "Tyranowski, whose own spiritual formation was based on the writings of St. John of the Cross and St. Teresa of Avila, helped me to read their works, something uncommon for a person my age" (*Gift and Mystery*, p. 24). Eventually he would write his doctoral thesis on the theology of St. John of the Cross. Increasingly, the pull of the priesthood—where he could preside over a very different kind of theater of the living Word—began to win out over acting.

One evening in February 1941, Karol returned home from work to discover the dead body of his father. His last close relation—and a man he had deeply loved and revered—was gone.

Wotyla was now living and interacting with people from all backgrounds and conditions—actors, intellectuals, religious, and working men, first in the stone quarry and then in the chemical plant where he still labored. The young man without a family became close to many working-class families. They would invite him to dinner and cover for him on the night shift to give him time to study. John Paul later jokingly referred to his experience as a "worker seminarian," in reference to the "worker priest" movement popular in Western Europe just before the war.

The year after his father died, Wotyla decided to become a priest. Studying with the theology faculty of the Jagiellonion University (which was being operated secretly), he continued to work at the chemical plant. In 1944, he moved, with several other seminarians, into the residence of Adam Stefan Sapieha, the Metropolitan Archbishop. The dangers he and the others courted by following their call were real: One of his classmates was grabbed by the Gestapo one night and ended up in front of a firing squad.

Accepting the Cross

In 1945, when the war ended, much of the world turned to rebuilding and achieving normalcy. But Poland, like the rest of Eastern Europe, had been "liberated" by the Soviet Union, which installed a puppet Communist government. Wotyla continued his priestly studies. His archbishop detected his promise and ordained him in November 1946, earlier than the rest of his class, so that he could be sent to Rome for a two-year doctoral program. Writing of his ordination fifty years later, John Paul recalled "lying prostrate on the floor with arms outstretched in the form of a cross, awaiting the moment of the imposition of hands" (*Gift and Mystery*. p. 43). In that rite, Wotyla saw himself, like the apostle Peter, accepting the cross of Christ in his own life and becoming the "floor" for others to walk over to guide their steps.

In 1948, Wotyla returned to his homeland, where he found the church struggling to care for her people's spiritual welfare and championing their human rights. "The two totalitarian systems which tragically marked our century—Nazism on the one hand, marked by the horrors of war and the concentration camps, and communism on the other, with its regime of oppression and terror—I came to know, so to speak, from within" (*Gift and Mystery*, p. 67). From these experiences would grow John Paul's deep concern for the dignity of every human person and the need to respect human rights.

Once again, he was to straddle different worlds. He took very seriously his pastoral duties and his relationships with working-class Poles, from whom he learned much about marriage, family life, and the everyday brand of heroism demanded of lay Catholics. He also taught at two universities, consolidating his ties with intellectuals and the students who, then as now, responded so well to him.

During this time, Wotyla further developed his philosophy of the human person, which underpins his way of looking at and explaining so many central modern issues, such as human rights and the sacredness of human life. As he would write years later in *Crossing the Threshold of Hope*, "The person is a being for whom the only suitable dimension is love. We are just to a person if we love him. This is as true for God as it is for man" (p. 201).

Wotyla's special intellectual, personal, and spiritual qualities were recognized first by the Polish hierarchy and then by Rome, as he was quickly put in positions of authority. In 1958, when he was only thirty-eight, he was made auxiliary bishop of Krakow. Four years later, he became administrator of the archdiocese, and in 1964, he was consecrated archbishop of Krakow. He attended all of the sessions of Vatican II and was especially active in the Council's *Declaration on Religious Freedom* and its *Pastoral Constitution on the Church in the Modern World*.

Even as the nation's ranking bishop, Wotyla found time for writing, teaching, mixing with all kinds of people—and many hours for prayer. In the midst of Communist roadblocks to the Church's mission to nourish the faith of the Poles, John Paul personified the firm courage with which he spoke his "Be Not Afraid" in St. Peter's Square in 1978. He negotiated new parishes and secretly ordained priests for nearby Czechoslovakia.

Energy and Vision

When Karol Wotyla became Pope John Paul II, he was a vigorous fifty-eight-year-old man, fond of skiing and kayaking. As the church's first non-Italian pope in over 450 years, and an accomplished linguist in at least seven languages, John Paul II had the background, energy, and vision to embark on a strenuous series of international trips. Twenty years and more than 100 foreign trips later, though weakened by old age, several operations, and the lingering effects of a would-be assassin's bullet in St. Peter's Square in 1981, he still travels the world. His appearances draw mammoth crowds of people who derive faith and courage from his own plentiful supply.

While his personal presence has been enormously effective, John Paul has also used his pen to preach Christ in encyclicals, books, and numerous apostolic letters and exhortations. One of his most important efforts to confirm and consolidate Catholic teaching at the end of this century was the commissioning of a new worldwide Catechism, the first since the Council of Trent.

Catholics and religious people focus principally on the Pope's evangelistic efforts, but even the secular world has been forced to acknowledge his influence. His articulation of human rights, his deft support of the Polish Solidarity movement, and his connection with the Polish people are widely recognized as being critical to the collapse of Communism in Eastern Europe.

As pope, John Paul's sure-footed, confident handling of the many modern "isms"—including secularism, totalitarianism, and moral relativism—is based on his assurance that God loves us unreservedly without in any way ignoring how far we must go to become what he intends. Made in God's image, we are destined for his heavenly home, but we must learn to love as he does: "*Man affirms himself most completely by giving of himself*" (*Crossing the Threshold of Hope*, p. 202).

Proclaiming the Truth

This explains what puzzles so many secular observers of John Paul II. They see his genuine openness, interest in others, engagement of people, experiences, and ideas, and at first they are lulled into thinking he is like them, with their toleration of all ideas as equally "valid." Then they run up against what they call his "rigidity" and "dogmatism." They cannot reconcile genuine acceptance of others with a need to proclaim the truth. But to this pope these two things are one. To truly love someone is to want his good and to be willing to give of yourself for his good. Knowledge of God, love of God, the journey toward union with God—we naturally seek these for those we love, if we have found them for ourselves.

People who have met John Paul II testify to how he lives his philosophy of personalism. Anyone speaking to him has his complete attention. John Paul actively and intensively focuses on those he meets, seeking to absorb both what is said and what is felt. This is one clue to John Paul's urgent desire for progress toward union with other Christian churches. Loving attention toward another while reverencing the truth—what better definition of ecumenism can we seek?

A courage strong enough to be hopeful in desperate circumstances, a powerful and wide-ranging intellect, a confident faith unafraid to engage others in pursuit of the truth in love, a determination to defend the rights of human beings infinitely precious to God their Father—these hallmarks of John Paul II have contributed to his powerful impact and significant achievements as successor to St. Peter.

"Every time Christ exhorts us to have no fear, He has both God and man in mind. He means: *Do not be afraid of God . . . Do not be afraid to say 'Father'!*" (*Crossing the Threshold of Hope*, p. 6). ∾

Forgiveness, Reconciliation, Mercy

THE "MOMENT OF FORGIVENESS"

Society can become "ever more human" only when we introduce into all the mutual relationships which form its moral aspect the moment of forgiveness, which is so much of the essence of the gospel. Forgiveness demonstrates the presence in the world of *the love which is more powerful than sin.* Forgiveness is also the fundamental condition for reconciliation, not only in the relationship of God with man, but also in relationships between people. A world from which forgiveness was eliminated would be nothing but a world of cold and unfeeling justice, in the name of which each person would claim his or her own rights *vis-a-vis* others; the various kinds of selfishness latent in man would transform life and human society into a system of oppression of the weak by the strong, or into an arena of permanent strife between one group and another.

Proclaiming the Mystery of Mercy

For this reason, the Church must consider it one of her principal duties—at every stage of history and especially in our modern age—*to proclaim and to introduce into life* the mystery of mercy, supremely revealed in Jesus Christ. Not only for the Church herself as the community of believers but also in a certain sense for all humanity, this mystery is the *source* of a life different from the life which can be built by man, who is exposed to the oppressive forces of the threefold concupiscence active within him (cf. 1 John 2:16). It is precisely in the name of this mystery that Christ teaches us to forgive always. How often we repeat the words of the prayer which he himself taught us, asking *"forgive us* our trespasses *as we forgive* those who trespass against us," which means those who are guilty of something in our regard (Matthew 6:12)! It is indeed difficult to express the profound value of the attitude which these words describe and inculcate. How many things these words say to every individual about others and also about himself! The consciousness of being trespassers against each other goes hand in hand with the call to fraternal solidarity, which St. Paul expressed in his concise exhortation to "forbear one another in love" (Ephesians 4:2, cf. Galatians 6:2). What a lesson of humility is to be found here with regard to man, with regard both to one's neighbor and to oneself! What a school of good will for daily living, in the various conditions of our existence! If we were to ignore this lesson, what would remain of any "humanist" program of life and education?

"Seventy Times Seven"

Christ emphasizes so insistently the need to forgive others that when Peter asked him how many times he should forgive his neighbor he answered with the symbolic number of "seventy times seven" (Matthew 18:22), meaning that he must be able to forgive everyone every time. It is obvious that such a generous requirement of *forgiveness does not cancel out* the objective *requirements of justice.* Properly understood, justice constitutes, so to speak, the goal of forgiveness. In no passage of the gospel message does forgiveness, or mercy as its source, mean indulgence towards evil, towards scandals, towards injury or insult. In any case, reparation for evil and scandal, compensation for injury, and satisfaction for insult are conditions for forgiveness. [1] ❦

BE RECONCILED TO GOD!

God is faithful to his eternal plan even when man, under the impulse of the evil one (cf. Wisdom 2:24) and carried away by his own pride, abuses the freedom given to him in order to love and generously seek what is good, and refuses to obey his Lord and Father. God is faithful even when man, instead of responding with love to God's love, opposes him and treats him like a rival, deluding himself and relying on his own power, with the resulting break of relationship with the one who created him. In spite of this transgression on man's part, God remains faithful in love. It is certainly true that the story of the Garden of Eden makes us think about the tragic consequences of rejecting the Father, which becomes evident in man's inner disorder and in the breakdown of harmony between man and woman, brother and brother (cf. Genesis 3:12; 4:16). Also significant is the gospel parable of the two brothers who, in different ways, distance themselves from their father and cause a rift between them. Refusal of God's fatherly love and of his loving gifts is always at the root of humanity's divisions.

God Is Rich in Mercy

But we know that God, "rich in mercy" (cf. Ephesians 2:4), like the father in the parable, does not close his heart to any of his children. He waits for them, looks for them, goes to meet them at the place where the refusal of communion imprisons them in isolation and division. He calls them to gather about his table in the joy of the feast of forgiveness and reconciliation.

This initiative on God's part is made concrete and manifest in the redemptive act of Christ, which radiates through the world by means of the ministry of the

Church. For, according to our faith, the Word of God became flesh and came to dwell in the world; he entered into the history of the world, summing it up and recapitulating it in himself (Ephesians 1:10). He revealed to us that God is love, and he gave us the "new commandment" of love (John 13:34), at the same time communicating to us the certainty that the path of love is open for all people, so that the effort to establish universal brotherhood is not a vain one. By conquering through his death on the cross evil and the power of sin, by his loving obedience, he brought salvation to all and became reconciliation for all. In him God reconciled man to himself.

The Church carries on the proclamation of reconciliation which Christ caused to echo through the villages of Galilee and all Palestine (cf. Mark 1:15) and does not cease to invite all humanity to be converted and to believe in the good news. She speaks in the name of Christ, making her own the appeal of St. Paul which we have already recalled: "We are ambassadors for Christ, God making his appeal through us. We beseech you on behalf of Christ, be reconciled to God" (cf. 2 Corinthians 5:20). [2] ◠

THE FACE OF MERCY

Love is transformed into mercy when it is necessary to go beyond the precise norm of justice—precise and often too narrow. The prodigal son, having wasted the property he received from his father, deserves—after his return—to earn his living by working in his father's house as a hired servant and possibly, little by little, to build up a certain provision of material goods, though perhaps never as much as the amount he had squandered. This would be demanded by the order of justice, especially as the son had not only squandered the part of the inheritance belonging to him but *had also hurt and offended his father* by his whole conduct. Since this conduct had in his own eyes deprived him of his dignity as a son, it could not be a matter of indifference to his father. It was bound to make him suffer. It was also bound to implicate him in some way. And yet, after all, it was his own son who was involved, and such a relationship could never be altered or destroyed by any sort of behavior. The prodigal son is aware of this and it is precisely this awareness that shows him clearly the dignity which he has lost and which makes him honestly evaluate the position that he could still expect in his father's house. [3]

A Faithful Father

This *exact picture of the prodigal son's state of mind enables us to understand exactly what the mercy of God consists in*. There is no doubt that in this simple but penetrating analogy the figure of the father reveals to us God as Father. The conduct of the father in the parable and his whole behavior, which manifests his internal attitude, enables us to rediscover the individual threads of the Old Testament vision of mercy in a synthesis which is totally new, full of simplicity and depth. The father of the prodigal son *is faithful to his fatherhood, faithful to the love* that he had always lavished on his son. This fidelity is expressed in the parable not only by his immediate readiness to welcome him home when he returns after having squandered his inheritance; it is expressed even more fully by that joy, that merrymaking for the squanderer after his return, merrymaking which is so generous that it provokes the opposition and hatred of the elder brother, who had never gone far away from his father and had never abandoned the home.

Agape Love

The father's fidelity to himself—a trait already known by the Old Testament term *hesed*—is at the same time expressed in a manner particularly charged with affection. We read, in fact, that when the father saw the prodigal son returning home "he had *compassion*, ran to meet him, threw his arms around his neck and kissed him" (Luke 15:20). He certainly does this under the influence of a deep affection, and this also explains his generosity towards his son, that generosity which so angers the elder son. Nevertheless, the causes of this emotion are to be sought at a deeper level. Notice, the father is aware that a fundamental good has been saved: the good of his son's humanity.

Although the son has squandered the inheritance, *nevertheless his humanity is saved.* Indeed, *it has been,* in a way, *found again.* The father's words to the elder son reveal this: "It was fitting to make merry and be glad, for this your brother was dead and is alive; he was lost and is found" (Luke 15:32). . . .

Mercy—as Christ has presented it in the parable of the prodigal son—has *the interior form of the love* that in the New Testament is called *agape.* This love is able to reach down to every prodigal son, to every human misery, and above all to every form of moral misery, to sin. When this happens, the person who is the object of mercy does not feel humiliated, but rather found again and "restored to value." The father first and foremost expresses to him his joy that he has been "found again" and that he has "returned to life." This joy indicates a good that has remained intact: even if he is a prodigal, a son does not cease to be truly his father's son; it also indicates a good that has been found again, which in the case of the prodigal son was his return to the truth about himself. . . .

Mercy: The Heart of the Gospel

The parable of the prodigal son expresses in a simple but profound way *the reality of conversion.* Conversion is the most concrete expression of the working of love and of the presence of mercy in the human world. The true and proper meaning of mercy does not consist only in looking, however penetratingly and compassionately, at moral, physical or material evil: mercy is manifested in its true and proper aspect when it restores to value, promotes and *draws good from all the forms of evil* existing in the world and in man. Understood in this way, mercy constitutes the fundamental content of the messianic message of Christ and the constitutive power of his mission. His disciples and followers understood and practiced mercy in the same way. Mercy never ceased to reveal itself, in their hearts and in their actions, as an especially creative proof of the love which does not allow itself to be "conquered by evil," but overcomes "evil with good" (cf. Romans 12:21). The genuine face of mercy has to be ever revealed anew. In spite of many prejudices, mercy seems particularly necessary for our times. [4] ∽

A Love That is "Greater Than Sin"

The cross on Calvary . . . is a fresh manifestation of the eternal fatherhood of God, who in [Christ] draws near again to humanity, to each human being, giving him the thrice holy "Spirit of truth" (cf. John 16:13).

This revelation of the Father and outpouring of the Holy Spirit, which stamp an indelible seal on the mystery of the Redemption, explain the meaning of the cross and death of Christ. The God of creation is revealed as the God of redemption, as the God who is "faithful to himself" (cf. 1 Thessalonians 5:24), and faithful to his love for man and the world, which he revealed on the day of creation. His is a love that does not draw back before anything that justice requires in him. Therefore "for our sake (God) made him (the Son) to be sin who knew no sin" (2 Corinthians 5:21; Galatians 3:13). If he "made to be sin" him who was without any sin whatever, it was to reveal the love that is always greater than the whole of creation, the love that is he himself, since "God is love" (1 John 4:8,16). Above all, love is greater than sin, than weakness, than the "futility of creation" (Romans 8:20); it is stronger than death; it is a love always ready to raise up and forgive, always ready to go to meet the prodigal son (Luke 15:11-32), always looking for "the revealing of the sons of God" (Romans 8:19), who are called "to the glory that is to be revealed" (cf. Romans 8:18). This revelation of love is also described as mercy; and in man's history this revelation of love and mercy has taken a form and a name: that of Jesus Christ. [5] ◎

Prayer and the Eucharist

THE HOLY SPIRIT, THE "BREATH" OF PRAYER

Wherever people are praying in the world, there the Holy Spirit is, the living breath of prayer. It is a beautiful and salutary thought to recognize that, if prayer is offered throughout the world, in the past, in the present and in the future, equally widespread is the presence and action of the Holy Spirit, who "breathes" prayer in the heart of man in all the endless range of the most varied situations and conditions, sometimes favorable and sometimes unfavorable to the spiritual and religious life. Many times, through the influence of the Spirit, prayer rises from the human heart in spite of prohibitions and persecutions and even official proclamations regarding the non-religious or even atheistic character of public life. Prayer always remains the voice of all those who apparently have no voice—and in this voice there always echoes *that "loud cry"* attributed to Christ by the Letter to the Hebrews (5:7). Prayer is also *the revelation* of that *abyss* which is the heart of man: a depth which comes *from God* and *which only God can fill*, precisely *with the Holy Spirit*. We read in Luke: "If you then, who are evil, know how to give good gifts to your children, how much more will the heavenly Father give the Holy Spirit to those who ask him" (11:13).

The Holy Spirit is the gift that comes into man's heart together *with prayer*. In prayer he manifests himself first of all and above all as the gift that "helps us in our weakness." This is the magnificent thought developed by St. Paul in the Letter to the Romans, when he writes: "For we do not know how to pray as we ought, but the Spirit himself intercedes for us with sighs too deep for words" (8:26). Therefore, the Holy Spirit not only enables us to pray, but guides us "from within" in prayer: he is present in our prayer and gives it a divine dimension (cf. Origen, *De Oratione*, 2). Thus *"he who searches the hearts of men knows what is the mind of the Spirit*, because the Spirit intercedes for the saints according to the will of God" (Romans 8:27). Prayer through the power of the Holy Spirit becomes the ever more mature expression of the new man, who by means of this prayer participates in the divine life.

A Revival of Prayer

Our difficult age has a special need of prayer. In the course of history—both in the past and in the present—many men and women have borne witness to the importance of prayer by consecrating themselves to the praise of God and to the life of prayer, especially in monasteries and convents. So, too, recent years have been seeing a growth in the number of people who, in ever more widespread movements and groups, are giving first place to prayer and seeking in prayer a renewal of their spiritual life. This is a significant and comforting sign, for from this experience there is coming a real contribution to the revival of prayer among the faithful, who have been helped to gain a clearer idea of the Holy Spirit as he who inspires in hearts a profound yearning for holiness.

In many individuals and many communities there is a growing awareness that, even with all the rapid progress of technological and scientific civilization, and despite the real conquests and goals attained, *man is threatened, humanity is threatened.* In the face of this danger, and indeed already experiencing the frightful reality of man's spiritual decadence, individuals and whole communities, guided as it were by an inner sense of faith, are seeking the strength to raise man up again, to save him from himself, from his own errors and mistakes that often make harmful his very conquests. And thus they are discovering prayer, in which the "Spirit who helps us in our weakness" manifests himself. In this way the times in which we are living are bringing the Holy Spirit closer to the many who are returning to prayer. [1] ❧

PRAYING AS A FAMILY

Family prayer has its own characteristic qualities. It is prayer offered *in common*, husband and wife together, parents and children together. Communion in prayer is both a consequence of and a requirement for the communion bestowed by the sacraments of Baptism and Matrimony. The words with which the Lord Jesus promises his presence can be applied to the members of the Christian family in a special way: "Again I say to you, if two of you agree on earth about anything they ask, it will be done for them by my Father in heaven. For where two or three are gathered in my name, there am I in the midst of them" (Matthew 18:19-20).

Family prayer has for its very own object *family life itself*. . . . Joys and sorrows, hopes and disappointments, births and birthday celebrations, wedding anniversaries of the parents, departures, separations and homecomings, important and far-reaching decisions, the death of those who are dear, etc.—all of these mark God's loving intervention in the family's history. They should be seen as suitable moments for thanksgiving, for petition, for trusting abandonment of the family into the hands of their common Father in heaven. The dignity and responsibility of the Christian family as the domestic Church can be achieved only with God's unceasing aid, which will surely be granted if it is humbly and trustingly petitioned in prayer. [2]

Discovering the Mystery of God

By reason of their dignity and mission, Christian parents have the specific responsibility of educating their children in prayer, introducing them to gradual discovery of the mystery of God and to personal dialogue with him: "It is particularly in the Christian family, enriched by the grace and the office of the sacrament of Matrimony, that from the earliest years children should be taught, according to the faith received in Baptism, to have a knowledge of God, to worship Him and to love their neighbor" (Vatican II, *Declaration on Christian Education*, 3).

The concrete example and living witness of parents is fundamental and irreplaceable in educating their children to pray. Only by praying together with their children can a father and mother—exercising their royal priesthood—penetrate the innermost depths of their children's hearts and leave an impression that the future events in their lives will not be able to efface. [3] ❧

CELEBRATING THE LORD'S DAY

All human life, and therefore all human time, must become praise of the Creator and thanksgiving to him. But man's relationship with God also *demands times of explicit prayer,* in which the relationship becomes an intense dialogue, involving every dimension of the person. "The Lord's Day" is the day of this relationship *par excellence* when men and women raise their song to God and become the voice of all creation.

This is precisely why it is also the *day of rest*. Speaking vividly as it does of "renewal" and "detachment," the interruption of the often oppressive rhythm of work expresses the dependence of man and the cosmos upon God. *Everything belongs to God!* The Lord's Day returns again and again to declare this principle within the weekly reckoning of time. The "Sabbath" . . . recalls that *the universe and history belong to God;* and without a constant awareness of that truth, man cannot serve in the world as co-worker of the Creator. [4]

The Risen Lord in Our Midst

"I am with you always, to the end of the age" (Matthew 28:20). This promise of Christ never ceases to resound in the Church as the fertile secret of her life and the wellspring of her hope. As the day of resurrection, Sunday is not only the remembrance of a past event: it is a celebration of the living presence of the Risen Lord in the midst of his own people.

For this presence to be properly proclaimed and lived, it is not enough that the disciples of Christ pray individually and commemorate the death and resurrection of Christ inwardly, in the secrecy of their hearts. Those who have received the grace of Baptism are not saved as individuals alone, but as members of the Mystical Body, having become part of the People of God (Vatican II, *Dogmatic Constitution on the Church*, 9). It is important therefore that they come together to express fully the very identity of the Church, the *ekklesia*, the assembly called together by the Risen Lord who offered his life "to reunite the scattered children of God" (John 11:52). They have become "one" in Christ (cf. Galatians 3:28) through the gift of the Spirit. This unity becomes visible when Christians gather together: it is then that they come to know vividly and to testify to the world that they are the people redeemed, drawn "from every tribe and language and people and nation" (Revelation 5:9). The assembly of Christ's disciples embodies from age to age the image of the first Christian community which Luke gives as an example in the Acts of the Apostles, when he recounts that the first baptized believers "devoted themselves to the apostles' teaching and fellowship, to the breaking of bread and the prayers" (2:42). [5] ⌬

THE SACRAMENT OF LOVE

Eucharistic worship constitutes the soul of all Christian life. In fact, Christian life is expressed in the fulfilling of the greatest commandment, that is to say, in the love of God and neighbor, and this love finds its source in the blessed Sacrament, which is commonly called the sacrament of love.

The Eucharist signifies this charity, and therefore recalls it, makes it present and at the same time brings it about. Every time that we consciously share in it, there opens in our souls a real dimension of that unfathomable love that includes everything that God has done and continues to do for us human beings, as Christ says: "My Father goes on working, and so do I" (John 5:17). Together with this unfathomable and free gift, which is charity revealed in its fullest degree in the saving sacrifice of the Son of God, the sacrifice of which the Eucharist is the indelible sign, there also springs up within us a lively response of love. We not only know love; we ourselves begin to love. We enter, so to speak, upon the path of love and along this path make progress. Thanks to the Eucharist, the love that springs up within us from the Eucharist develops in us, becomes deeper and grows stronger.

Eucharistic worship is therefore precisely the expression of that love which is the authentic and deepest characteristic of the Christian vocation. This worship springs from the love and serves the love to which we are all called in Jesus Christ. A living fruit of this worship is the perfecting of the image of God that we bear within us, an image that corresponds to the one that Christ has revealed in us. As we thus become adorers of the Father "in spirit and truth"

(John 4:23), we mature in an ever fuller union with Christ, we are ever more united to him, and—if one may use the expression—we are ever more in harmony with him. [6]

The Source of Charity

The authentic sense of the Eucharist becomes of itself the school of active love for neighbor. We know that this is the true and full order of love that the Lord has taught us: "By this love you have for one another, everyone will know that you are my disciples" (John 13:35). The Eucharist educates us to this love in a deeper way; it shows us, in fact, what value each person, our brother or sister, has in God's eyes, if Christ offers himself equally to each one, under the species of bread and wine. If our Eucharistic worship is authentic, it must make us grow in awareness of the dignity of each person. The awareness of that dignity becomes the deepest motive of our relationship with our neighbor.

We must also become particularly sensitive to all human suffering and misery, to all injustice and wrong, and seek the way to redress them effectively. Let us learn to discover with respect the truth about the inner self that becomes the dwelling place of God present in the Eucharist. Christ comes into the hearts of our brothers and sisters and visits their consciences. How the image of each and every one changes, when we become aware of this reality, when we make it the subject of our reflections! The sense of the Eucharistic Mystery leads us to a love for our neighbor, to a love for every human being. [7]

Since therefore the Eucharist is the source of charity, it has always been at the center of the life of Christ's disciples. It has the appearance of bread and wine, that is to say of food and drink; it is therefore as familiar to people, as closely linked to their life, as food and drink. The veneration of God, who is love, springs, in eucharistic worship, from that kind of intimacy in which he himself, by analogy with food and drink, fills our spiritual being, ensuring its life, as food and drink do. This "eucharistic" veneration of God therefore strictly corresponds to his saving plan. He himself, the Father, wants the "true worshipers" (John 4:23) to worship him precisely in this way, and it is Christ who expresses this desire, both with his words and likewise with this sacrament in which he makes possible worship of the Father in the way most in conformity with the Father's will. [8] ∽

UNITED WITH JESUS IN THE EUCHARIST

The Eucharist is the center and summit of the whole of sacramental life, through which each Christian receives the saving power of the Redemption, beginning with the mystery of Baptism, in which we are buried into the death of Christ, in order to become sharers in his resurrection (cf. Romans 6:3-5), as the Apostle teaches. In the light of this teaching, we see still more clearly the reason why the entire sacramental life of the Church and of each Christian reaches its summit and fullness in the Eucharist. For by Christ's will there is in this sacrament a continual renewing of the mystery of the sacrifice of himself that Christ offered to the Father on the altar of the cross, a sacrifice that the Father accepted, giving, in return for this total self-giving by his Son, who "became obedient unto death" (Philippians 2:8), His own paternal gift, that is to say the grant of new immortal life in the resurrection, since the Father is the first source and the giver of life from the beginning. That new life, which involves the bodily glorification of the crucified Christ, became an efficacious sign of the new gift granted to humanity, the gift that is the Holy Spirit, through whom the divine life that the Father has in himself and gives to his Son (cf. John 5:26; 1 John 5:11) is communicated to all men who are united with Christ.

Becoming Children of God

The Eucharist is the most perfect sacrament of this union. By celebrating and also partaking of the Eucharist we unite ourselves with Christ on earth and in heaven who intercedes for us with the Father

(Hebrews 9:24; 1 John 2:1) but we always do so through the redeeming act of his sacrifice, through which he has redeemed us, so that we have been "bought with a price" (1 Corinthians 6:20). The "price" of our redemption is likewise a further proof of the value that God himself sets on man and of our dignity in Christ. For by becoming "children of God" (John 1:12) adopted sons (cf. Romans 8:23), we also become in his likeness "a kingdom and priests" and obtain "a royal priesthood" (Revelation 5:10; 1 Peter 2:9), that is to say we share in that unique and irreversible restoration of man and the world to the Father that was carried out once for all by him, who is both the eternal Son and also true Man. The Eucharist is the sacrament in which our new being is most completely expressed and in which Christ himself unceasingly and in an ever new manner "bears witness" in the Holy Spirit to our spirit (cf. 1 John 5:5-11) that each of us, as a sharer in the mystery of the Redemption, has access to the fruits of the filial reconciliation with God (cf. Romans 5:10-11; 2 Corinthians 5:18-19; Colossians 1:20,22) that he himself actuated and continually actuates among us by means of the Church's ministry.

The Eucharist Builds the Church

It is an essential truth, not only of doctrine but also of life, that the Eucharist builds the Church (Vatican II, *Dogmatic Constitution on the Church*, 11), building it as the authentic community of the People of God, as the assembly of the faithful, bearing the same mark of unity that was shared by the apostles and the first disciples of the Lord. The Eucharist builds ever anew this community and unity, ever building and regenerating it on the basis of the sacrifice of Christ, since it commemorates his death on the cross (Vatican II, *Constitution on the Sacred Liturgy*, 47), the price by which he redeemed us. Accordingly, in the Eucharist we touch in a way the very mystery of the body and blood of the Lord, as is attested by the very words used at its institution, the words that, because of that institution, have become the words with which those called to this ministry in the Church unceasingly celebrate the Eucharist. [9]

Marriage and Family

THE BRIDEGROOM IS WITH YOU

At the beginning of his mission, we find Jesus at *Cana in Galilee,* taking part in a wedding banquet, together with Mary and with the first disciples (cf. John 2:1-11). He thus wishes to make clear *to what extent the truth about the family is part of God's Revelation and the history of salvation.* In the Old Testament, and particularly in the Prophets, we find many beautiful expressions about the *love of God.* It is a gentle love like that of a mother for her child, a tender love like that of the bridegroom for his bride, but at the same time an equally and intensely jealous love. It is not in the first place a love which chastises but one which forgives; a love which deigns to meet man just as the father does in the case of the prodigal son; a love which raises him up and gives him a share in divine life. It is an amazing love: something entirely new and previously unknown to the whole pagan world.

At Cana in Galilee Jesus is, as it were, the *herald of the divine truth about marriage*, that truth on which the human family can rely, gaining reassurance amid all the trials of life.

The Radical Demands of Love

Jesus proclaims this truth by his presence at the wedding in Cana and by working his first "sign": water changed into wine. Jesus proclaims the truth about marriage again when, speaking to the Pharisees, he explains how the love which comes from God, a tender and spousal love, *gives rise to profound and radical demands*. Moses, by allowing a certificate of divorce to be drawn up, had been less demanding. When in their lively argument the Pharisees appealed to Moses, Jesus' answer was categorical: "from the beginning it was not so" (Matthew 19:8). And he reminds them that the One who created man created him male and female, and ordained that "a man leaves his father and his mother and cleaves to his wife, and they become one flesh" (Genesis 2:24). With logical consistency Jesus concludes: "So they are no longer two but one flesh. What therefore God has joined together, let not man put asunder" (Matthew 19:6). To the objection of the Pharisees who vaunt the Law of Moses he replies: "For your hardness of heart Moses allowed you to divorce your wives, but from the beginning it was not so" (Matthew 19:8).

Jesus appeals to "the beginning," seeing at the very origins of creation God's plan, on which the family is based, and, through the family, the entire history of humanity. What marriage is in nature becomes, by the will of Christ, a true sacrament of the New Covenant, sealed by the blood of Christ the Redeemer. *Spouses and families, remember at what price you have been "bought"* (cf. 1 Corinthians 6:20)!

But it is *humanly difficult* to accept and to live this marvelous truth. Should we be surprised that Moses relented before the insistent demands of his fellow Israelites, if the apostles themselves, upon hearing the words of the Master, reply by saying: "If such is the case of a man with his wife, it is not expedient to marry" (Matthew 19:10)! Nonetheless, in view of the good of man and woman, of the family and the whole of society, Jesus confirms the demand which God laid down from the beginning. . . .

It is in the family where living stones are formed for that spiritual house spoken of by the Apostle Peter (cf. 1 Peter 2:5). The bodies of the husband and wife are the dwelling-place of the Holy Spirit (cf. 1 Corinthians 6:19). Because the transmission of divine life presumes the transmission of human life, marriage not only brings about the birth of human children, but also, through the power of Baptism, the birth of adopted children of God, who live the new life received from Christ through his Spirit.

Protected by the Good Shepherd

Dear brothers and sisters, spouses and parents, this is how the *Bridegroom is with you.* You know that he is the Good Shepherd. You know who he is, and you know his voice. You know where he is leading you, and how he strives to give you pastures where you can find life and find it in abundance. You know how he withstands the marauding wolves, and is ever ready to rescue his sheep: every husband and wife, every son and daughter, every member of your families. You know that he, as the Good Shepherd, is prepared to lay down his own life for his flock (cf. John 10:11). He leads you by paths which are not the steep and treach-erous paths of many of today's ideologies, and he repeats to today's world the fullness of truth, even as he did in his conversation with the Pharisees or when he announced it to the apostles, who then proclaimed it to all the ends of the earth and to all the people of their day, to Jews and Greeks alike. The disciples were fully conscious that Christ had made all things new. They knew that man had been made a "new creation": no longer Jew or Greek, no longer slave or free, no longer male or female, but "one" in Christ (cf. Galatians 3:28) and endowed with the dignity of an adopted child of God. On the day of Pentecost man received the Spirit, the Comforter, the Spirit of truth. This was the beginning of the new People of God, the Church, the foreshadowing of new heavens and a new earth (cf. Revelation 21:1).

The apostles, overcoming their initial fears even about marriage and the family, grew in courage. They came to understand that marriage and family are a true vocation which comes from God himself and is an apostolate: the apostolate of the laity. Families are meant to contribute to the transformation of the earth and the renewal of the world, of creation and of all humanity.

Do Not Be Afraid!

Dear families, you too should be fearless, ever ready to give witness to the hope that is in you (cf. 1 Peter 3:15), since the Good Shepherd has put that hope in your hearts through the gospel. You should be ready to follow Christ towards the pastures of life, which he himself has prepared through the Paschal Mystery of his Death and Resurrection.

Do not be afraid of the risks! God's strength is always far more powerful than your difficulties! Immeasurably greater than the evil at work in the world is the power of the *Sacrament of Reconciliation*, which the Fathers of the Church rightly called a "second Baptism." Much more influential than the corruption present in the world is the divine power of the Sacrament of *Confirmation*, which brings Baptism to its maturity. And incomparably greater than all is the power of the Eucharist.

The *Eucharist* is truly a wondrous sacrament. In it Christ has given us himself as food and drink, as a source of saving power. He has left himself to us that we might have life and have it in abundance (cf. John 10:10): the life which is in him and which he has shared with us by the gift of the Spirit in rising from the dead on the third day. The life that comes from

Christ is a life for us. *It is for you, dear husbands and wives, parents and families!* Did Jesus not institute the Eucharist in a family-like setting during the Last Supper? When you meet for meals and are together in harmony, *Christ is close to you.* And he is Emmanuel, God with us, in an even greater way whenever you approach the table of the Eucharist. It can happen, as it did at Emmaus, that he is recognized only in "the breaking of the bread" (cf. Luke 24:35). It may well be that he is knocking at the door for a long time, waiting for it to be opened so that he can enter and eat with us (cf. Revelation 3:20). The Last Supper and the words he spoke there contain all the power and wisdom of the sacrifice of the Cross. No other power and wisdom exist by which we can be saved and through which we can help to save others. There is no other power and no other wisdom by which you, parents, can educate both your children and yourselves. The *educational power of the Eucharist* has been proved down the generations and centuries.

The Source of our Hope and Strength

Everywhere the Good Shepherd is with us. Even as he was at Cana in Galilee, *the Bridegroom in the midst of the bride and groom* as they entrusted themselves to each other for their whole life, so the Good Shepherd is also with us today as the reason for our hope, the source of strength for our hearts, the well-spring of ever new enthusiasm and the sign of the triumph of the "civilization of love." Jesus, the Good Shepherd, continues to say to us: *Do not be afraid. I am with you.* "I am with you always, to the close of the age" (Matthew 28:20). What is the source of this strength? What is the reason for our certainty that you are with us, even though they put you to death, O Son of God, and you died like any other human being? What is the reason for this certainty? The Evangelist says: "He loved them to the end" (John 13:1). Thus do you love us, you who are the First and the Last, the Living One; you who died and are alive forevermore (cf. Revelation 1:17-18). [1]

THE "SACRED REALITY" OF FAMILY

The bond that unites a family is not only a matter of natural kinship or of shared life and experience. It is essentially a holy and religious bond. Marriage and the family are sacred realities.

The sacredness of Christian marriage consists in the fact that in God's plan the marriage covenant between a man and a woman becomes the image and symbol of the covenant which unites God and his people (cf. Hosea 2:21; Jeremiah 3:6-13, Isaiah 54:5-10). It is the sign of Christ's love for his Church (cf. Ephesians 5:32). Because God's love is faithful and irrevocable, so those who have been married "in

Christ" are called to remain faithful to each other forever. Did not Jesus himself say to us: "What therefore God has joined together, let no man put asunder" (cf. Matthew 19:6)?

Open to the Holy Spirit

Contemporary society has a special need of the witness of couples who persevere in their union as an eloquent, even if sometimes suffering, "sign" in our human condition of the steadfastness of God's love. Day after day Christian married couples are called to open their hearts ever more to the Holy Spirit, whose power never fails and who enables them to love each other as Christ has loved us. And, as St. Paul writes to the Galatians, "the fruit of the spirit is love, joy, peace, patient endurance, kindness, generosity, faith, mildness and chastity" (Galatians 5:22-23). All of this constitutes the rule of life and the program of personal development of Christian couples. And each Christian community has a great responsibility to sustain couples in their love.

From such love Christian families are born. In them children are welcomed as a splendid gift of God's goodness, and they are educated in the essential values of human life, learning above all that "man is more precious for what he is than for what he has" (cf. Vatican II, *Pastoral Constitution on the Church in the Modern World*, 35). The entire family endeavors to practice respect for the dignity of every individual and to offer disinterested service to those in need.

The Domestic Church

Christian families exist to form a communion of persons in love. As such, the Church and the family are each in its own way living representations in human history of the eternal loving communion of the three persons of the Most Holy Trinity. In fact, the family is called the Church in miniature, "the domestic church," a particular expression of the Church through the human experience of love and common life. Like the Church, the family ought to be a place where the gospel is transmitted and from which the gospel radiates to other families and to the whole of society. [2]

A SPIRIT OF SACRIFICE

All members of the family, each according to his or her own gift, have the grace and responsibility of building, day by day, the communion of persons, making the family "a school of deeper humanity" (Vatican II, *Pastoral Constitution on the Church in the Modern World*, 52): this happens where there is care and love for the little ones, the sick, the aged; where there is mutual service every day; when there is a sharing of goods, of joys and of sorrows. . . .

Family communion can only be preserved and perfected through a great spirit of sacrifice. It requires, in fact, a ready and generous openness of each and all to understanding, to forbearance, to pardon, to reconciliation. There is no family that does not know how selfishness, discord, tension and conflict violently attack and at times mortally wound its own communion: hence there arise the many and varied forms of division in family life. But, at the same time, every family is called by the God of peace to have the joyous and renewing experience of "reconciliation," that is, communion reestablished, unity restored. In particular, participation in the sacrament of Reconciliation and in the banquet of the one Body of Christ offers to the Christian family the grace and the responsibility of overcoming every division and of moving towards the fullness of communion willed by God, responding in this way to the ardent desire of the Lord: "that they may be one" (John 17:21).[3] ∾

To the Youth of the World

YOU ARE THE CHILDREN OF THE LIGHT

"You are the light of the world. . . Your light must shine before all." (Matthew 5:14-16)

Dear Young People,

Ask yourselves: Do I believe these words of Jesus in the gospel? Jesus is calling you the light of the world. He is asking you to let your light shine before others. I know that in your hearts you want to say: "Here I am, Lord. Here I am. I come to do your will" (cf. Hebrews 10:7). But only if you are one with Jesus can you share his light and be a light to the world.

Are you ready for this?

Sadly, too many people today are living apart from the light—in a world of illusions, a world of fleeting shadows and promises unfulfilled. If you look to Jesus, if you live the Truth that is Jesus, you will have in you the light that reveals the truths and values on which to build your own happiness, while building a world of justice, peace and solidarity. Remember what Jesus said: "I am the light of the world; those who follow me will not walk in darkness, but will have the light of life" (cf. John 8:12).

Because Jesus is the Light, we too become light when we proclaim him. This is the heart of the Christian mission to which each of you has been called through Baptism and Confirmation. You are called to make the light of Christ shine brightly in the world.

Darkness and Light

When you were little, were you sometimes afraid of the dark? Today you are no longer children afraid of the dark. You are teenagers and young adults. But already you realize that there is another kind of darkness in the world: the darkness of doubt and uncertainty. You may feel the darkness of loneliness and isolation. Your anxieties may come from questions about your future, or regrets about past choices.

Sometimes the world itself seems filled with darkness. The darkness of children who go hungry and even die. The darkness of homeless people who lack work and proper medical care. The darkness of violence: violence against the unborn child, violence in families, the violence of gangs, the violence of sexual abuse, the violence of drugs that destroy the body, mind and heart. There is something terribly wrong when so many young people are overcome by hopelessness to the point of taking their own lives. And already in parts of this nation, laws have been passed which allow doctors to end the lives of the very people they are sworn to help. God's gift of life is being rejected. Death is chosen over life, and this brings with it the darkness of despair.

But you believe in the light (cf. John 12:36)! Do not listen to those who encourage you to lie, to shirk responsibility, to put yourselves first. Do not listen to those who tell you that chastity is *passé*. In your hearts you know that true love is a gift from God and respects his plan for the union of man and woman in marriage. Do not be taken in by false values and deceptive slogans, especially about your freedom. True freedom is a wonderful gift from God, and it has been a cherished part of your country's history. But when freedom is separated from truth, individuals lose their moral direction and the very fabric of society begins to unravel.

Freedom is not the ability to do anything we want, whenever we want. Rather, freedom is the ability to live responsibly the truth of our relationship with God and with one another. Remember what Jesus said: "You will know the truth and the truth will set you free" (John 8:32). Let no one mislead you or prevent you from seeing what really matters. Turn to Jesus, listen to him, and discover the true meaning and direction of your lives.

Meeting Jesus

You are children of the light (cf. John 12:36)! You belong to Christ, and he has called you by name. Your first responsibility is to get to know as much as you can about him, in your parishes, in religious instruction in your high schools and colleges, in your youth groups and Newman Centers.

But you will get to know him truly and personally only through prayer. What is needed is that you talk to him, and listen to him.

Today we are living in an age of instant communications. But do you realize what a unique form of communication prayer is? Prayer enables us to meet God at the most profound level of our being. It connects us directly to God: Father, Son and Holy Spirit, in a constant exchange of love.

Through prayer you will learn to become the light of the world, because in prayer you become one with the source of our true light, Jesus himself.

Open Your Hearts

Each of you has a special mission in life, and you are each called to be a disciple of Christ. Many of you will serve God in the vocation of Christian married life; some of you will serve him as dedicated single persons; some as priests and religious. But all of you must be the light of the world. To those of you who think that Christ may be inviting you to follow him in the priesthood or the consecrated life I make this personal appeal: I ask you to open your hearts generously to him; do not delay your response. The Lord will help you to know his will; he will help you to follow your vocation courageously.

Young friends, in the days and weeks and years

ahead, for as long as you remember this evening, remember that the Pope came to the United States, to the City of St. Louis, to call the young people of America to Christ, to invite you to follow him. He came to challenge you to be the light of the world! "The light shines in the darkness and the darkness does not overcome it" (John 1:5). Jesus who has conquered sin and death reminds you: "I am with you always" (Matthew 28:20). He says: "Courage! It is I; have no fear" (Mark 6:50).

On the horizon of this city stands the Gateway Arch, which often catches the sunlight in its different colors and hues. In a similar way, in a thousand different ways, you must reflect the light of Christ through your lives of prayer and joyful service of others. With the help of Mary, the Mother of Jesus, the young people of America will do this magnificently!

Remember: Christ is calling you; the Church needs you; the Pope believes in you and he expects great things of you!

Praised be Jesus Christ! [1]

Go, and Proclaim the Good News!

Christ first invites, then he reveals himself more fully, and then he sends. He invites in order to make himself known to those whom he wishes to send. He sends those who have come to know the mystery of his person and of his kingdom. For the gospel must be proclaimed through the power of their witness. And the strength of their witness depends on knowledge and love of Jesus Christ himself. Every apostle must be able to identify with what the First Letter of John says: "This is what we proclaim to you: What was from the beginning, what we have heard, what we have seen with our eyes, what we have looked upon and our hands have touched—we speak of the word of life" (1 John 1:1).

That same gospel experience penetrates the whole World Youth Day. The young people who are gathering here from all parts of the world are involved in a similar process: at some point Christ entered your lives and invited you to a greater awareness of your baptismal consecration; with God's grace and the help of a believing community you grew in understanding of your Christian identity and your role in the Church and in society. As mature Catholics, you began to take an active part in the apostolate. . . .

Christ the Lord is at the very heart of the World Youth Day, and he continues to invite many young people to join him in the sublime task of spreading his kingdom. He is here because the Church is here. He is here in the Eucharist, and through the ministry of his priests and bishops, in union with the successor of Peter. Christ is here through the faith and love of so many young people who have prepared themselves spiritually for this meeting and have worked hard and made sacrifices in order to be able to make this pilgrimage of hope and commitment. . . .

The New Evangelization

Have no fear! Denver, like the previous World Youth Days, is a time of grace: a great gathering of young people, all speaking different languages but all united in proclaiming the mystery of Christ and of the new life he gives. This is especially evident in the catecheses being given each day in various languages. In prayer and song, so many different tongues ring out in praise of God. All this makes Denver a reflection of what happened in Jerusalem at Pentecost (cf. Acts 2:1-4). Out of all the diversity of the young people gathered here—diversity or origin, race and language—the Spirit of truth will create the deep and abiding unity of commitment to the new evangelization, in which the defense of human life, the promotion of human rights and the fostering of a civilization of love are urgent tasks.

To be committed to the new evangelization means that we are convinced that we have something of value to offer to the human family at the dawn of the new millennium. All of us who have come here—young people and their pastors, bishops and the pope—must be aware that it is not enough to offer a "merely human wisdom, a pseudo-science of well-being" (*Redemptoris Missio*, 11). We must be convinced that we have a "pearl of great price" (cf.

Matthew 13:46), a great "treasure" (cf. Matthew 13:44), which is fundamental to the earthly existence and eternal salvation of every member of the human race. . . .

We know that Christ never abandons his Church. At a time like this, when many are confused regarding the fundamental truths and values on which to build their lives and seek their eternal salvation, when many Catholics are in danger of losing their faith—the pearl of great price—when there are not enough priests, not enough religious sisters and brothers to give support and guidance, not enough contemplative religious to keep before the people's eyes the sense of the absolute supremacy of God, we must be convinced that Christ is knocking at many hearts, looking for young people like you to send into the vineyard, where an abundant harvest is ready.

But we—we human beings—have this treasure in earthen vessels (cf. 2 Corinthians 4:7). That is why we are often afraid of the demands of the Redeemer's love. We may try to appease our conscience by giving of ourselves, but in limited and partial ways, or in ways that we like—not always in the ways that the Lord suggests. Yet, the fact that we carry this treasure in earthen vessels serves to make it clear that "its surpassing power comes from God and not from us" (2 Corinthians 4:7). Wherever young men and women allow the grace of Christ to work in them and produce new life, the extraordinary power of divine love is released into their lives and into the life of the community. It transforms their attitude and behavior and inevitably attracts others to follow the same adventurous path. This power comes from God and not from us.

Here Am I! Send Me!

The one who had invited you to Denver, and who can call you at any stage of your pilgrimage through life, wants you to have the treasure of knowing him more fully. He wants to occupy the central place in your hearts, and therefore he purifies your love and tests your courage. The realization of his hidden but certain presence acts like a burning coal that touches your lips (cf. Isaiah 6:7) and makes you able to repeat the eternal Yes of the Son, as the Letter to the Hebrews says: "Then I said, 'As it is written of me in the book, I have come to do your will, O God'" (Hebrews 10:7). That Yes guided every step of the Son of Man: "Jesus said to them, 'Truly, truly, I say to you, the Son can do nothing of his own accord, but only what he sees the Father doing'" (John 5:19). And Mary gave the very same Yes to God's plan for her life: "Let it be done to me as you say" (Luke 1:38).

Christ is asking the young people of the World Youth Day: "Whom shall I send" (Isaiah 6:8)?

And, with fervor, let each one respond: "Here am I! Send me" (Isaiah 6:8)!

Do not forget the needs of your homelands! Heed the cry of the poor and the oppressed in the countries and continents from which you come! Be convinced that the gospel is the only path of genuine liberation and salvation for the world's peoples: "Your salvation, O Lord, is for all the peoples" (Responsorial Psalm).

Everyone who, in response to Christ's invitation, comes to Denver to take part in the World Youth Day must hear his words: "Go . . . and proclaim the good news" (Mark 16:15).

Let us earnestly pray the Lord of the harvest that the youth of the world will not hesitate to reply: "Here am I! Send me!" "Send us!" Amen. [2] ❧

DISCOVERING GOD'S PLAN

A human being is *a creature* and at the same time an adopted child of God in Christ; *he is a child of God.* Hence during youth a person puts the question, "What must I do?" not only to himself and to other people from whom he can expect an answer, especially his parents and teachers, but he *puts it* also *to God, as his Creator and Father.* He puts it in the context of this particular interior sphere in which he has learned to be in a close relationship with God, above all *in prayer.* He therefore asks God: "What must I do?", what is your plan for my life? Your creative, fatherly plan? *What is your will?* I wish to do it.

In this context, the "plan" takes on the meaning of a "life vocation," as something which is *entrusted by God to an individual as a task.* Young people, entering into themselves and at the same time entering into conversation with Christ in prayer, desire as it were *to read the eternal thought* which God the Creator and Father has in their regard. They then become convinced that the task assigned to them by God *is left completely to their own freedom*, and at the same time is determined by various circumstances of an interior and exterior nature. Examining these circumstances, the young person, boy or girl, constructs his or her plan of life and at the same time *recognizes* this plan *as the vocation to which God is calling him or her.*

A Life Vocation

I desire therefore to entrust to all of you, the young people to whom this Letter is addressed, this marvelous task which is linked with the discovery before God of each one's life vocation. This is an exciting task. It is a *fascinating interior undertaking.* In this undertaking your humanity develops and grows, while your young personality acquires ever greater inner maturity. You become rooted in that which each of you is, in order to become *that which you must become: for yourself—for other people—for God.*

Parallel with the process of discovering one's own "life vocation" there should also be a progressively clearer realization of how this life vocation is at the same time a "Christian vocation". . . .

Every human life vocation as a Christian vocation corresponds to the evangelical call. *Christ's "Follow me" makes itself heard on the different paths* taken by the disciples and confessors of the divine Redeemer. There are different ways of becoming imitators of Christ—*not only* by bearing witness to the eschatological kingdom of truth and love, *but also* by striving to bring about the transformation of the whole of temporal reality according to the spirit of the gospel. [3] ❧

The Call to Unity

READING THE SIGNS OF THE TIMES

Ut *Unum Sint!* The call for Christian unity made by the Second Vatican Ecumenical Council with such impassioned commitment is finding an ever greater echo in the hearts of believers, especially as the Year 2000 approaches, a year which Christians will celebrate as a sacred Jubilee, the commemoration of the Incarnation of the Son of God, who became man in order to save humanity.

The courageous witness of so many martyrs of our century, including members of churches and ecclesial communities not in full communion with the Catholic Church, gives new vigor to the Council's call and reminds us of our duty to listen to and put into practice its exhortation. These brothers and sisters of ours, united in the selfless offering of their lives for the kingdom of God, are the most powerful proof that every factor of division can be transcended and overcome in the total gift of self for the sake of the gospel. [1]

A Call to Conversion

At the Second Vatican Council, the Catholic Church committed herself *irrevocably* to following the path of the ecumenical venture, thus heeding the Spirit of the Lord, who teaches people to interpret carefully the "signs of the times." The experiences of these years have made the Church even more profoundly aware of her identity and her mission in history. The Catholic Church acknowledges and confesses *the weaknesses of her members*, conscious that their sins are so many betrayals of and obstacles to the accomplishment of the Savior's plan. Because she feels herself constantly called to be renewed in the spirit of the gospel, she does not cease to do penance. At the same time, she acknowledges and exalts still more *the power of the Lord*, who fills her with the gift of holiness, leads her forward, and conforms her to his Passion and Resurrection. [2]

The unity of all divided humanity is the will of God. For this reason he sent his Son, so that by dying and rising for us he might bestow on us the Spirit of love. On the eve of his sacrifice on the cross, Jesus himself prayed to the Father for his disciples and for all those who believe in him, that they *might be one*, a living communion. This is the basis not only of the duty, but also of the responsibility before God and his plan, which falls to those who through Baptism become members of the Body of Christ, a Body in which the fullness of reconciliation and communion must be made present. How is it possible to remain divided, if we have been "buried" through Baptism in the Lord's death, in the very act by which God, through the death of his Son, has broken down the walls of division? Division "openly contradicts the will of Christ, provides a stumbling block to the world, and inflicts damage on the most holy cause of proclaiming the good news to every creature" (Vatican II, *Decree on Ecumenism*, 1). [3]

We proceed along the road leading to the conversion of hearts guided by love which is directed to God and, at the same time, to all our brothers and sisters, including those not in full communion with us. Love gives rise to the desire for unity, even in those who have never been aware of the need for it. Love builds communion between individuals and between communities. If we love one another, we strive to deepen our communion and make it perfect. *Love is given to God* as the perfect source of communion—the unity of Father, Son and Holy Spirit—that we may draw from that source the strength to build communion between individuals and communities, or to re-establish it between Christians still divided. Love is the great undercurrent which gives life and adds vigor to the movement toward unity. [4]

Receiving the Grace of Unity

The power of God's Spirit gives growth and builds up the Church down the centuries. As the Church turns her gaze to the new millennium, she asks the Spirit for the grace to strengthen her own unity and to make it grow toward full communion with other Christians.

How is the Church to obtain this grace? In the first place, through *prayer*. Prayer should always concern itself with the longing for unity, and as such is one of the basic forms of our love for Christ and for the Father who is rich in mercy. In this journey which we are undertaking with other Christians toward the new millennium prayer must occupy the first place.

How is she to obtain this grace? Through *giving thanks*, so that we do not present ourselves empty-handed at the appointed time: "Likewise the Spirit helps us in our weakness . . . [and] intercedes for us with sighs too deep for words" (Romans 8:26), disposing us to ask God for what we need.

How is she to obtain this grace? Through *hope* in the Spirit, who can banish from us the painful memories of our separation. The Spirit is able to grant us clear-sightedness, strength and courage to take whatever steps are necessary, that our commitment may be ever more authentic.

And should we ask if all this is possible, the answer will always be yes. It is the same answer which Mary of Nazareth heard: with God nothing is impossible. [5] ⟨∾⟩

THE GRACE OF PERSEVERANCE

There are people who in the face of the difficulties or because they consider that the first ecumenical endeavors have brought negative results would have liked to turn back. Some even express the opinion that these efforts are harmful to the cause of the gospel, are leading to a further rupture in the Church, are causing confusion of ideas in questions of faith and morals and are ending up with a specific indifferentism. It is perhaps a good thing that the spokesmen for these opinions should express their fears. However, in this respect also, correct limits must be maintained.

It is obvious that this new stage in the Church's life demands of us a faith that is particularly aware, profound and responsible. True ecumenical activity means openness, drawing closer, availability for dialogue, and a shared investigation of the truth in the full evangelical and Christian sense; but in no way does it or can it mean giving up or in any way diminishing the treasures of divine truth that the Church has constantly confessed and taught.

To all who, for whatever motive, would wish to dissuade the Church from seeking the universal unity of Christians the question must once again be put: Have we the right not to do it? Can we fail to have trust—in spite of all human weakness and all the faults of past centuries—in our Lord's grace as revealed recently through what the Holy Spirit said and we heard during the Council? If we were to do so, we would deny the truth concerning ourselves that was so eloquently expressed by the Apostle: "By the grace of God I am what I am, and his grace towards me was not in vain" (1 Corinthians 15:10). [6] ∽

UNITY—A GIFT FROM GOD

The commitment to ecumenism is of primary importance for the Christian. It is in fact known that Jesus prayed at the Last Supper for the unity of his disciples, with heartfelt intensity: "As you, Father are in me, and I in you, I pray that they may be [one] in us, that the world may believe that you sent me" (John 17:21).

Jesus did not hesitate to pray to the Father for his disciples "that their unity may be complete" (John 17:23) in spite of the difficulties and tensions he knew they would encounter. He himself had noticed the disagreements and tensions he knew they would encounter. He himself had noticed the disagreements between the Twelve even during the Last Supper, and foresaw those which were shortly to appear in the life of the Christian communities, scattered throughout such a vast and varied world. Nonetheless, he prayed for the complete unity of his followers and for this end he offered the sacrifice of his own life.

Unity is, therefore, a gift of the Lord to his Church,

"a people gathered together by the unity of the Father, the Son and the Holy Spirit" as St. Cyprian effectively points out. Indeed, "the highest exemplar and source of this mystery is the unity, in the Trinity of Persons, of one God, the Father and the Son in the Holy Spirit" (Vatican II, *Decree on Ecumenism*, 2).

In reality, in the first community that gathered after Pentecost, we see that deep unity prevailed: all "devoted themselves to the Apostles' instruction and the communal life, to the breaking of bread and the prayers" (Acts 2:42); and "the community of believers were of one heart and one mind" (Acts 4:32). . . .

A Painful History

The New Testament writings themselves tell us that from the very beginning of the Church's life there have been divisions among Christians. . . . From the painful confrontation of this historical situation with the gospel law of unity, the ecumenical movement arose, a movement which aims at restoring even visible unity among all Christians, "that the world may be converted to the gospel and so be saved, to the glory of God" (Vatican II, *Decree on Ecumenism*, 1). The Second Vatican Council gave the greatest importance to this movement, pointing out how it implies, for those who work for it, a communion of faith in the Trinity and in Christ, and a common longing for the one and universal Church (*Decree on Ecumenism*, 1). But authentic ecumenical commitment likewise requires of all Christians, motivated by a sincere desire for communion, freedom from prejudices which hinder the development of the dialogue of charity in truth. . . .

United As One Body

We must note further that, according to the Council, those who are separated from the Catholic Church preserve a certain communion—incomplete but real—with her. In fact, those who believe in Christ and have received Baptism, are rightly recognized by the children of the Catholic Church "as brothers in the Lord," even if there are differences "whether in doctrine and sometimes in discipline, or concerning the structure of the Church" (*Decree on Ecumenism*, 3). We can be united with them through several elements of great value, such as, "the written Word of God; the life of grace; faith, hope and charity, with the other interior gifts of the Holy Spirit, as well as visible elements" (*Decree on Ecumenism*, 3).

Even with regard to the work of evangelization and sanctification, the Council's attitude is sincere and respectful. It affirms that the churches and ecclesial communities are not in fact deprived of significance and importance in the mystery of salvation. "For the Spirit of Christ has not refrained from using them as means of salvation" (*Decree on Ecumenism*, 3).

All this contains the impelling appeal for full

unity. It is not merely a matter of gathering up all the spiritual riches scattered throughout the Christian communities, as if in so doing we might arrive at a more perfect Church, the Church God would desire for the future. Instead, it is a question of bringing about fully that Church which God already manifested in her profound reality at Pentecost. This is the goal towards which all must strive, already united in hope, prayer, conversion of heart, and as is often demanded of us, in suffering which draws its value from the cross of Christ. [7] ❧

UNITY THROUGH PRAYER

When Christians pray together, the goal of unity seems closer. The long history of Christians marked by many divisions seems to converge once more because it tends toward that Source of its unity which is Jesus Christ. He "is the same yesterday, today and forever!" (Hebrews 13:8). In the fellowship of prayer Christ is truly present; he prays "in us," "with us," and "for us." It is he who leads our prayer in the Spirit-Consoler whom he promised and then bestowed on his Church in the Upper Room in Jerusalem, when he established her in her original unity.

Along the ecumenical path to unity, pride of place

certainly belongs to common prayer, the prayerful union of those who gather together around Christ himself. If Christians, despite their divisions, can grow ever more united in *common prayer* around Christ, they will grow in the awareness of how little divides them in comparison to what unites them. If they meet more often and more regularly before Christ in prayer, they will be able to gain the courage to face all the painful human reality of their divisions, and they will find themselves together once more in that community of the Church which Christ constantly builds up in the Holy Spirit, in spite of all weaknesses and human limitations. [8]

Children of One Father

Prayer, the community at prayer, enables us always to discover anew the evangelical truth of the words: *"You have one Father"* (Matthew 23:9), the Father—Abba—invoked by Christ himself, the Only-begotten and Consubstantial Son. And again: *"You have one teacher, and you are all brethren"* (Matthew 23:8). "Ecumenical" prayer discloses this fundamental dimension of brotherhood in Christ, who died to gather together the children of God who were scattered, so that in becoming "sons and daughters in the Son" (cf. Ephesians 1:5) we might show forth more fully both the mysterious reality of God's fatherhood and the truth about the human nature shared by each and every individual.

"Ecumenical" prayer, as the prayer of brothers and sisters, expresses all this. Precisely because they are separated from one another, they meet in Christ with all the more hope, *entrusting to him the future of their unity and their communion.* Here too we can appropriately apply the teaching of the Council: "The Lord Jesus, when he prayed to the Father *'that all may be one...as we are one'* (John 17:21-22), opened up vistas closed to human reason. For he implied a certain likeness between the union of the Divine Persons, and the union of God's children in truth and charity" (Vatican II, *Pastoral Constitution on the Church in the Modern World,* 24).

The change of heart which is the essential condition for every authentic search for unity flows from prayer and its realization is guided by prayer. [9]

A Witness to Prayer

Praying for unity is not a matter reserved only to those who actually experience the lack of unity among Christians. In the deep personal dialogue which each of us must carry on with the Lord in prayer, concern for unity cannot be absent. Only in this way, in fact, will that concern fully become part of the reality of our life and of the commitments we have taken on in the Church. It was in order to reaffirm this duty that I set before the faithful of the Catholic Church a model which I consider exemplary, the model of a Trappistine Sister, *Blessed Maria Gabriella of Unity*, whom I beatified on January 25, 1983. Sister Maria Gabriella, called by her vocation to be apart from the world, devoted her life to meditation and prayer centered on chapter seventeen of St. John's Gospel, and offered her life for Christian unity. This is truly the cornerstone of all prayer: the total and unconditional offering of one's life to the Father, through the Son, in the Holy Spirit. The example of Sister Maria Gabriella is instructive; it helps us to understand that there are no special times, situations or places of prayer for unity. Christ's prayer to the Father is offered as a model for everyone, always and everywhere. [10]

Made in the Image of God

THE WAY TO SELF-DISCOVERY

Man cannot live without love. He remains a being that is incomprehensible for himself, his life is senseless, if love is not revealed to him, if he does not encounter love, if he does not experience it and make it his own, if he does not participate intimately in it. This, as has already been said, is why Christ the Redeemer "fully reveals man to himself." If we may use the expression, this is the human dimension of the mystery of the redemption. In this dimension man finds again the greatness, dignity and value that belong to his humanity. In the mystery of the redemption man becomes newly "expressed" and, in a way, is newly created. He is newly created! "There is neither Jew nor Greek, there is neither slave nor free, there is neither male nor female; for you are all one in Christ Jesus" (Galatians 3:28).

The man who wishes to understand himself thoroughly—and not just in accordance with immediate, partial, often superficial, and even illusory standards and measures of his being—he must with his unrest, uncertainty and even his weakness and sinfulness, with his life and death, draw near to Christ. He must, so to speak, enter into him with all his own self, he must "appropriate" and assimilate the whole of the reality of the Incarnation and Redemption in order to find himself. If this profound process takes place within him, he then bears fruit not only of adoration of God but also of deep wonder at himself. How precious must man be in the eyes of the Creator, if he "gained so great a Redeemer" (*Exsultet at the Easter Vigil*), and if God "gave his only Son" in order that man "should not perish but have eternal life" (cf. John 3:16).

The Certainty of Faith

In reality, the name for that deep amazement at man's worth and dignity is the gospel, that is to say: the good news. It is also called Christianity. This amazement determines the Church's mission in the world and, perhaps even more so, "in the modern world." This amazement, which is also a conviction and a certitude—at its deepest root it is the certainty of faith, but in a hidden and mysterious way it vivifies every aspect of authentic humanism—is closely connected with Christ. It also fixes Christ's place—so to speak, his particular right of citizenship—in the history of man and mankind. Unceasingly contemplating the whole of Christ's mystery, the Church knows with all the certainty of faith that the redemption that took place through the cross has definitively restored his dignity to man and given back meaning to his life in the world, a meaning that was lost to a considerable extent because of sin. And for that reason, the redemption was accomplished in the paschal mystery, leading through the cross and death to resurrection. [1] ◎

IN THE HANDS OF A LOVING GOD

Man's life comes from God; it is his gift, his image and imprint, a sharing in his breath of life. God therefore *is the sole Lord of this life:* man cannot do with it as he wills. God himself makes this clear to Noah after the flood: "For your own lifeblood, too, I will demand an accounting . . . and from man in regard to his fellow man I will demand an accounting for human life" (Genesis 9:5). The biblical text is concerned to emphasize how the sacredness of life has its foundation in God and in his creative activity: "For God made man in his own image" (Genesis 9:6).

Human life and death are thus in the hands of God, in his power: "In his hand is the life of every living thing and the breath of all mankind," exclaims Job (12:10). "The Lord brings to death and brings to life; he brings down to Sheol and raises up" (1 Samuel 2:6). He alone can say: "It is I who bring both death and life" (Deuteronomy 32:39).

But God does not exercise this power in an arbitrary

and threatening way, but rather as part of his *care and loving concern for his creatures*. If it is true that human life is in the hands of God, it is no less true that these are loving hands, like those of a mother who accepts, nurtures and takes care of her child: "I have calmed and quieted my soul, like a child quieted at its mother's breast; like a child that is quieted is my soul" (Psalm 131:2; cf. Isaiah 49:15; 66:12-13; Hosea 11:4). Thus Israel does not see in the history of peoples and in the destiny of individuals the outcome of mere chance or of blind fate, but rather the results of a loving plan by which God brings together all the possibilities of life and opposes the powers of death arising from sin: "God did not make death, and he does not delight in the death of the living. For he created all things that they might exist" (Wisdom 1:13-14). [2]

An Incomparable Dignity

"Before I formed you in the womb I knew you, and before you were born I consecrated you" (Jeremiah 1:5): *the life of every individual, from its very beginning, is part of God's plan.* Job, from the depth of his pain, stops to contemplate the work of God who miraculously formed his body in his mother's womb. Here he finds reason for trust, and he expresses his belief that there is a divine plan for his life: "You have fashioned and made me; will you then turn and destroy me? Remember that you have made me of clay; and will you turn me to dust again? Did you not pour me out like milk and curdle me like cheese? You clothed me with skin and flesh, and knit me together with bones and sinews. You have granted me life and steadfast love; and your care has preserved my spirit" (Job 10:8-12). Expressions of awe and wonder at God's intervention in the life of a child in its mother's womb occur again and again in the Psalms (see, for example, Psalms 22:10-11; 71:6; 139:13-14).

How can anyone think that even a single moment of this marvelous process of the unfolding of life could be separated from the wise and loving work of the Creator, and left prey to human caprice? Certainly the mother of the seven brothers did not think so; she professes her faith in God, both the source and guarantee of life from its very conception, and the foundation of the hope of new life beyond death: "I do not know how you came into being in my womb. It was not I who gave you life and breath, nor I who set in order the elements within each of you. Therefore the Creator of the world, who shaped the beginning of man and devised the origin of all things, will in his mercy give life and breath back to you again, since you now forget yourselves for the sake of his laws" (2 Maccabees 7:22-23). [3]

Jesus: The Gospel of Life

Jesus is the only Gospel: we have nothing further to say or any other witness to bear.

To proclaim Jesus is itself to proclaim life. For Jesus is "the word of life" (1 John 1:1). In him "life was made manifest" (1 John 1:2); he himself is "the eternal life which was with the Father and was made manifest to us" (1 John 1:2). By the gift of the Spirit, this same life has been bestowed on us. It is in being destined to life in its fullness, to "eternal life," that every person's earthly life acquires its full meaning.

Enlightened by this *Gospel of life*, we feel a need to proclaim it and to bear witness to it in all its *marvelous newness*. Since it is one with Jesus himself, who makes all things new and conquers the "oldness" which comes from sin and leads to death, this gospel exceeds every human expectation and reveals the sublime heights to which the dignity of the human person is raised through grace. This is how St. Gregory of Nyssa understands it: "Man, as a being, is of no account; he is dust, grass, vanity. But once he is adopted by the God of the universe as a son, he becomes part of the family of that Being, whose excellence and greatness no one can see, hear or understand. What words, thoughts or flight of the spirit can praise the superabundance of this grace? Man surpasses his nature: mortal, he becomes immortal; perishable, he becomes imperishable; fleeting, he becomes eternal; human, he becomes divine" (*De Beatitudinibus*, Oratio VII).

Gratitude and joy at the incomparable dignity of man impel us to share this message with everyone: "that which we have seen and heard we proclaim also to you, so that you may have fellowship with us" (1 John 1:3). We need to bring the *Gospel of life* to the heart of every man and woman and to make it penetrate every part of society. [4]

The Face of Christ

This involves above all proclaiming *the core* of this gospel. It is the proclamation of a living God who is close to us, who calls us to profound communion with himself and awakens in us the certain hope of eternal life. It is the affirmation of the inseparable connection between the person, his life and his bodiliness. It is the presentation of human life as a life of relationship, a gift of God, the fruit and sign of his love. It is the proclamation that Jesus has a unique relationship with every person, which enables us to see in every human face the face of Christ. It is the call for a "sincere gift of self" as the fullest way to realize our personal freedom. [5] ⟨⟩

SHARING IN THE WORK
OF THE CREATOR

The word of God's revelation is profoundly marked by the fundamental truth that *man*, created in the image of God, *shares by his work in the activity of the Creator* and that, within the limits of his own human capabilities, man in a sense continues to develop that activity, and perfects it as he advances further and further in the discovery of the resources and values contained in the whole of creation. We find this truth at the very beginning of Sacred Scripture, in the book of Genesis, where the creation activity itself is presented in the form of "work" done by God during "six days" (cf. Genesis 2:2), "resting" on the seventh day (cf. Genesis 2:3). Besides, the last book of Sacred Scripture echoes the same respect for what God has done through his creative "work" when it proclaims: "Great and wonderful are your deeds, O Lord God the Almighty" (Revelation 15:3); this is similar to the book of Genesis, which concludes the description of each day of creation with the statement: "And God saw that it was good" (Genesis 1:4,10,12,18,21,25,31).

The Gospel of Work

This description of creation, which we find in the very first chapter of the book of Genesis, is also *in a sense the first "gospel of work."* For it shows what the dignity of work consists of: it teaches that man ought to imitate God, his Creator, in working, because man alone has the unique characteristic of likeness to God. Man ought to imitate God both in working and also in resting, since God himself wished to present his own creative activity under the form of *work and rest.*

This activity by God in the world always continues, as the words of *Christ attest: "My Father is working still . . ."* (John 5:17): He works with creative power by sustaining in existence the world that he called into being from nothing, and he works with salvific power in the hearts of those whom from the beginning he has destined for "rest" (cf. Hebrews 4:1,9-10) in union with himself in his "Father's house" (John 14:2). Therefore man's work too not only requires a rest every "seventh day" (cf. Deuteronomy 5:12-14, Exodus 20:8-12), but also cannot consist in the mere exercise of human strength in external action; it must leave room for man to prepare himself, by becoming more and more what in the will of God he ought to be, for the *"rest" that the Lord reserves for his servants and friends* (cf. Matthew 25:21).

Awareness that man's work is a participation in God's activity ought to permeate, as the Council teaches, even *"the most ordinary everyday activities.* For, while providing the substance of life for themselves and their families, men and women are performing their activities in a way which appropriately benefits society. They can justly consider that by their labor they are unfolding the Creator's work, consulting the advantages of their brothers and sisters, and contributing by their personal industry to the realization in history of the divine plan" (Vatican II, *Pastoral Constitution on the Church in the Modern World*, 34).

This Christian spirituality of work should be a heritage shared by all. Especially in the modern age, the *spirituality* of work should show the *maturity* called for by the tensions and restlessness of mind and heart. [6] ❧

THE MYSTERY OF HUMAN SUFFERING

As a result of Christ's salvific work, man exists on earth *with the hope* of eternal life and holiness. And even though the victory over sin and death achieved by Christ in his cross and resurrection does not abolish temporal suffering from human life, nor free from suffering the whole historical dimension of human existence, it nevertheless *throws a new light* upon this dimension and upon every suffering: the light of salvation. This is the light of the gospel, that is, of the good news. At the heart of this light is the truth expounded in the conversation with Nicodemus: "For God so loved the world that he gave his only Son" (John 3:16). This truth radically changes the picture of man's history and his earthly situation: in spite of the sin that took root in this history both as an original inheritance and as the "sin of the world" and as the sum of personal sins, God the Father has loved the only-begotten Son, that is, he loves him in a lasting way; and then in time, precisely through this all-surpassing love, he "gives" this Son, that he may strike at the very roots of human evil and thus draw close in a salvific way to the whole world of suffering in which man shares. [7]

In his messianic activity in the midst of Israel, Christ drew increasingly closer *to the world of human suffering*. "He went about doing good" (Acts 10:38), and his actions concerned primarily those who were suffering and seeking help. He healed the sick; consoled the afflicted; fed the hungry; freed people from deafness, from blindness, from leprosy, from the devil and from various physical disabilities; three times he restored the dead to life. He was sensitive to every human suffering, whether of the body or of the soul. And at the same time he taught, and at the heart of his teaching there are *the eight beatitudes*, which are addressed to people tried by various sufferings in their temporal life. These are "the poor in spirit" and "the afflicted" and "those who hunger and thirst for justice" and those who are "persecuted for justice' sake," when they insult them, persecute them and speak falsely every kind of evil against them for the sake of Christ (cf. Matthew 5:3-11). . . .

Suffering and the Cross

Christ drew close above all to the world of human suffering through the fact of having taken *this suffering upon his very self*. During his public activity, he experienced not only fatigue, homelessness, misunderstanding even on the part of those closest to him, but, more than anything, he became progressively more and more isolated and encircled by hostility and the preparations for putting him to death. Christ is aware of this, and often speaks to his disciples of the sufferings and death that await him: "Behold, we are going up to Jerusalem; and the Son of man *will be delivered* to the chief priests and the scribes, and they will condemn him to death and deliver him to the Gentiles; and they will mock him, and spit upon him, and scourge him, and kill him; and after three days he will rise" (Mark 10:33-34). Christ goes towards his passion and death with full awareness of the mission that he has to fulfill precisely in this way. Precisely *by means of this suffering* he must bring it about "that man should not perish, but have eternal life." Precisely by means of his cross he must strike at the roots of evil, planted in the history of man and in human souls. Precisely by means of his cross he must accomplish *the work of salvation*. This work in the plan of eternal Love has a redemptive character. [8]

Human suffering has reached its culmination in the passion of Christ. And at the same time it has entered into a completely new dimension and a new order: *it has been linked to love*, to that love of which Christ spoke to Nicodemus, to that love which creates good, drawing it out by means of suffering, just as the supreme good of the Redemption of the world was drawn from the cross of Christ, and from that cross constantly takes its beginning. The cross of Christ has become a source from which flow rivers of living water (cf. John 7:37-38). [9] ∽

The Mission of the Church

GO AND PREACH THE GOSPEL

The entire mission of the Church . . . is concentrated and manifested in *evangelization*. Through the winding passages of history the Church has made her way under the grace and the command of Jesus Christ: "Go into all the world and preach the gospel to the whole creation" (Mark 16:15). ". . . and lo, I am with you always, until the close of the age" (Matthew 28:20). "To evangelize," writes Paul VI, "is the grace and vocation proper to the Church, her most profound identity" (*Evangelii Nuntiandi*, 14).

Through evangelization the Church is built up into a *community of faith*: more precisely, into a community that *confesses* the faith in full adherence to the Word of God which is *celebrated* in the sacraments and *lived* in charity, the principle of Christian moral existence. In fact, the "good news" is directed to stirring a person to a conversion of heart and life and a clinging to Jesus Christ as Lord and Savior; to disposing a person to receive Baptism and the Eucharist and to strengthen a person in the prospect and realization of new life according to the Spirit.

Certainly the command of Jesus: "Go and preach the gospel" always maintains its vital value and its ever-pressing obligation. Nevertheless, the *present situation*, not only of the world but also of many parts of the Church, *absolutely demands that the word of Christ receive a more ready and generous obedience*. Every disciple is personally called by name; no disciple can withhold making a response: "Woe to me if I do not preach the gospel" (1 Corinthians 9:16). [1]

Meeting the Challenges

At this moment the lay faithful, in virtue of their participation in the prophetic mission of Christ, are fully part of this work of the Church. Their responsibility, in particular, is to testify how the Christian faith constitutes the only fully valid response—consciously perceived and stated by all in varying degrees—to the problems and hopes that life poses to every person and society. This will be possible if the lay faithful will know how to overcome in themselves the separation of the gospel from life, to again take up in their daily activities in family, work and society, an integrated approach to life that is fully brought about by the inspiration and strength of the gospel.

Listening to Christ

To all people of today, I once again repeat the impassioned cry with which I began my pastoral ministry: *"Do not be afraid! Open, indeed, open wide the doors to Christ!* Open to his saving power the confines of states, and systems political and economic, as well as the vast fields of culture, civilization, and development. Do not be afraid! Christ knows 'what is inside a person.' Only he knows! Today too often people do not know what they carry inside, in the deepest recesses of their soul, in their heart. Too often people are uncertain about a sense of life on earth. Invaded by doubts they are led into despair. Therefore—with humility and trust I beg and implore you—allow Christ to speak to the person in you. Only he has the words of life, yes, eternal life" (*Homily of Pope John Paul II*, October 22, 1978).

Opening wide the doors to Christ, accepting him into humanity itself poses absolutely no threat to persons, indeed it is the only road to take to arrive at the total truth and the exalted value of the human individual.

This vital synthesis will be achieved when the lay faithful know how to put the gospel and their daily duties of life into a most shining and convincing testimony, where, not fear but the loving pursuit of Christ and adherence to him will be the factors determining how a person is to live and grow, and these will lead to new ways of living more in conformity with human dignity.

Humanity is loved by God! This very simple yet profound proclamation is owed to humanity by the Church. Each Christian's words and life must make this proclamation resound: God loves you, Christ came for you, Christ is for you "the Way, the Truth and the Life!" (John 14:6). [2]

A "Great Venture"

The whole Church, pastors and lay faithful alike, standing on the threshold of the Third Millennium, ought to feel more strongly the Church's responsibility to obey the command of Christ, "Go into all the world and preach the gospel to the whole creation" (Mark 16:15), and take up anew the missionary endeavor. A great venture, both challenging and wonderful, is entrusted to the Church—that of a *re-evangelization*, which is so much needed by the present world. The lay faithful ought to regard themselves as an active and responsible part of this venture, called as they are to proclaim and to live the gospel in service to the person and to society while respecting the totality of the values and needs of both. [3] ∞

THE RICHES OF CHRIST ARE FOR EVERYONE

Jesus Christ is the stable principle and fixed center of the mission that God himself has entrusted to man. We must all share in this mission and concentrate all our forces on it, since it is more necessary than ever for modern mankind. If this mission seems to encounter greater opposition nowadays than ever before, this shows that today it is more necessary than ever and, in spite of the opposition, more awaited than ever. Here we touch indirectly on the mystery of the divine "economy" which linked salvation and grace with the cross.

It was not without reason that Christ said that "the kingdom of heaven has suffered violence, and men of violence take it by force" (Matthew 11:12) and moreover that "the children of this world are more astute. . .than are the children of light" (Luke 16:8). We gladly accept this rebuke, that we may be like those "violent people of God" that we have so often seen in the history of the Church and still see today, and that we may consciously join in the great mission of revealing Christ to the world, helping each person to find himself in Christ, and helping the contemporary generations of our brothers and sisters, the peoples, nations, states, mankind, developing countries and countries of opulence—in short, helping everyone to get to know "the unsearchable riches of Christ" (Ephesians 3:8), since these riches are for every individual and are everybody's property. [4] ⬯

THE NEW EVANGELIZATION—
PROCLAIMING THE MORAL TRUTH

Evangelization is the most powerful and stirring challenge which the Church has been called to face from her very beginning. Indeed, this challenge is posed not so much by the social and cultural milieu which she encounters in the course of history, as by the mandate of the Risen Christ, who defines the very reason for the Church's existence: "Go into all the world and preach the gospel to the whole creation" (Mark 16:15).

At least for many peoples, however, the present time is instead marked by a formidable challenge to undertake a "new evangelization," a proclamation of the gospel which is always new and always the bearer of new things, an evangelization which must be "new in its ardor, methods and expression" (*Address of Pope John Paul II to Bishops*, March 9, 1983).

Dechristianization, which weighs heavily upon entire peoples and communities once rich in faith and Christian life, involves not only the loss of faith or in any event its becoming irrelevant for everyday life, but also, and of necessity, *a decline or obscuring of the moral sense*. This comes about both as a result of a loss of awareness of the originality of gospel morality and as a result of an eclipse of fundamental principles and ethical values themselves. Today's widespread tendencies towards subjectivism, utilitarianism and relativism appear not merely as pragmatic attitudes or patterns of behavior, but rather as approaches having a basis in theory and claiming full cultural and social legitimacy. [5]

A New "Way"

Evangelization—and therefore the "new evangelization"—*also involves the proclamation and presentation of morality.* Jesus himself, even as he preached the kingdom of God and its saving love, called people to faith and conversion (cf. Mark 1:15). And when Peter, with the other apostles, proclaimed the Resurrection of Jesus of Nazareth from the dead, he held out a new life to be lived, a "way" to be followed, for those who would be disciples of the Risen One (cf. Acts 2:37-41; 3:17-20).

Just as it does in proclaiming the truths of faith, and even more so in presenting the foundations and content of Christian morality, the new evangelization will show its authenticity and unleash all its missionary force when it is carried out through the gift not only of the word proclaimed but also of the word lived. In particular, *the life of holiness* which is resplendent in so many members of the People of God, humble and often unseen, constitutes the simplest and most attractive way to perceive at once the beauty of truth, the liberating force of God's love, and the value of unconditional fidelity to all the demands of the

Lord's law, even in the most difficult situations. For this reason, the Church, as a wise teacher of morality, has always invited believers to seek and to find in the saints, and above all in the Virgin Mother of God "full of grace" and "all-holy," the model, the strength and the joy needed to live a life in accordance with God's commandments and the beatitudes of the gospel. [6]

The Spirit of Christ

At the heart of the new evangelization and of the new moral life which it proposes and awakens by its fruits of holiness and missionary zeal, there is the *Spirit of Christ*, the principle and strength of the fruitfulness of Holy Mother Church. As Pope Paul VI reminded us: "Evangelization will never be possible without the action of the Holy Spirit" (*Evangelii Nuntiandi*, 64). The Spirit of Jesus, received by the humble and docile heart of the believer, brings about the flourishing of Christian moral life and the witness of holiness amid the great variety of vocations, gifts, responsibilities, conditions and life situations. As Novatian once pointed out—here expressing the authentic faith of the Church—it is the Holy Spirit "who confirmed the hearts and minds of the disciples, who revealed the mysteries of the gospel, who shed upon them the light of things divine. Strengthened by his gift, they did not fear either prisons or chains for the name of the Lord; indeed they even trampled upon the powers and torments of the world, armed and strengthened by him, having in themselves the gifts which this same Spirit bestows and directs like jewels to the Church, the Bride of Christ. It is in fact he who raises up prophets in the Church, instructs teachers, guides tongues, works wonders and healings, accomplishes miracles, grants the discernment of spirits, assigns governance, inspires counsels, distributes and harmonizes every other charismatic gift. In this way he completes and perfects the Lord's Church everywhere and in all things" (*De Trinitate*, 29). [7] ☙

OPEN THE DOORS TO CHRIST!

Peoples everywhere, open the doors to Christ! His gospel in no way detracts from man's freedom, from the respect that is owed to every culture and to whatever is good in each religion. By accepting Christ, you open yourselves to the definitive Word of God, to the One in whom God has made himself fully known and has shown us the path to himself.

The number of those who do not know Christ and do not belong to the Church is constantly on the increase. Indeed, since the end of the Council it has almost doubled. When we consider this immense portion of humanity which is loved by the Father and for whom he sent his Son, the urgency of the Church's mission is obvious.

New Opportunities

Our own times offer the Church new opportunities in this field: we have witnessed the collapse of oppressive ideologies and political systems; the opening of frontiers and the formation of a more united world due to an increase in communications; the affirmation among peoples of the gospel values which Jesus made incarnate in his own life (peace, justice, brotherhood, concern for the needy); and a kind of soulless economic and technical development which only stimulates the search for the truth about God, about man and about the meaning of life itself.

God is opening before the Church the horizons of a humanity more fully prepared for the sowing of the gospel. I sense that the moment has come to commit all of the Church's energies to a new evangelization and to the mission *ad gentes*. No believer in Christ, no institution of the Church can avoid this supreme duty: to proclaim Christ to all peoples. [8]

"I Am Not Ashamed"

While respecting the beliefs and sensitivities of all, we must first clearly affirm our faith in Christ, the one Savior of mankind, a faith we have received as a gift from on high, not as a result of any merit of our own. We say with Paul, "I am not ashamed of the gospel: it is the power of God for salvation to everyone who has faith" (Romans 1:16). Christian martyrs of all times—including our own—have given and continue to give their lives in order to bear witness to this faith, in the conviction that every human being needs Jesus Christ, who has conquered sin and death and reconciled humanity to God.

Confirming his words by miracles and by his resurrection from the dead, Christ proclaimed himself to be the Son of God dwelling in intimate union with the Father, and was recognized as such by his disciples. The Church offers humanity the gospel, that prophetic message which responds to the needs and aspirations of the human heart and always remains "Good News." The Church cannot fail to proclaim that Jesus came to reveal the face of God and to merit salvation for all humanity by his cross and resurrection.

The Promise of New Life

To the question, "why mission?" we reply with the Church's faith and experience that true liberation consists in opening oneself to the love of Christ. In him, and only in him, are we set free from all alienation and doubt, from slavery to the power of sin and death. Christ is truly "our peace" (Ephesians 2:14); "the love of Christ impels us" (2 Corinthians 5:14), giving meaning and joy to our life. Mission is an issue of faith, an accurate indicator of our faith in Christ and his love for us.

The temptation today is to reduce Christianity to merely human wisdom, a pseudo-science of well-being. In our heavily secularized world a "gradual secularization of salvation" has taken place, so that people strive for the good of man, but man who is truncated, reduced to his merely horizontal dimension. We know, however, that Jesus came to bring integral salvation, one which embraces the whole person and all humanity, and opens up the wondrous prospect of divine filiation. Why mission? Because to us, as to St. Paul, "this grace was given, to preach to the Gentiles the unsearchable riches of Christ" (Ephesians 3:8). Newness of life in him is the "Good News" for men and women of every age: all are called to it and destined for it. Indeed, all people are searching for it, albeit at times in a confused way, and have a right to know the value of this gift and to approach it freely. The Church, and every individual Christian within her, may not keep hidden or monopolize this newness and richness which has been received from God's bounty in order to be communicated to all humankind.

This is why the Church's mission derives not only from the Lord's mandate but also from the profound demands of God's life within us. Those who are incorporated in the Catholic Church ought to sense their privilege and for that very reason their greater obligation of bearing witness to the faith and to the Christian life as a service to their brothers and sisters and as a fitting response to God. [9]

Evangelizing by Example

People today put more trust in witnesses than in teachers, in experience than in teaching, and in life and action than in theories. The witness of a Christian life is the first and irreplaceable form of mission: Christ, whose mission we continue, is the "witness" par excellence (Revelation 1:5; 3:14) and the model of all Christian witness. The Holy Spirit accompanies the Church along her way and associates her with the witness he gives to Christ (cf. John 15:26-27).

The first form of witness is the very life of the missionary, of the Christian family, and of the ecclesial community, which reveal a new way of living. The missionary who, despite all his or her human limitations and defects, lives a simple life, taking Christ as the model, is a sign of God and of transcendent realities. But everyone in the Church, striving to imitate the Divine Master, can and must bear this kind of witness; in many cases it is the only possible way of being a missionary.

The evangelical witness which the world finds most appealing is that of concern for people, and of charity toward the poor, the weak and those who suffer. The complete generosity underlying this attitude and these actions stands in marked contrast to human self-ishness. It raises precise questions which lead to God and to the gospel. A commitment to peace, justice, human rights and human promotion is also a witness to the gospel when it is a sign of concern for persons and is directed toward integral human development. [10]

The Witness of Love

Christians and Christian communities are very much a part of the life of their respective nations and can be a sign of the gospel in their fidelity to their native land, people and national culture, while always preserving the freedom brought by Christ. Christianity is open to universal brotherhood, for all men and women are sons and daughters of the same Father and brothers and sisters in Christ.

The Church is called to bear witness to Christ by taking courageous and prophetic stands in the face of the corruption of political or economic power; by not seeking her own glory and material wealth; by using her resources to serve the poorest of the poor and by imitating Christ's own simplicity of life. The Church and her missionaries must also bear the witness of humility, above all with regard to themselves—a humility which allows them to make a personal and communal examination of conscience in order to correct in their behavior whatever is contrary to the gospel and disfigures the face of Christ. [11]

Love and Justice

SEEING CHRIST IN THE POOR

The social message of the gospel must not be considered a theory, but above all else a basis and a motivation for action. Inspired by this message, some of the first Christians distributed their goods to the poor, bearing witness to the fact that, despite different social origins, it was possible for people to live together in peace and harmony. Through the power of the gospel, down the centuries monks tilled the land, men and women religious founded hospitals and shelters for the poor, confraternities as well as individual men and women of all states of life devoted themselves to the needy and to those on the margins of society, convinced as they were that Christ's words "as you did it to one of the least of these my brethren, you did it to me" (Matthew 25:40) were not intended to remain a pious wish, but were meant to become a concrete life commitment.

Today more than ever, the Church is aware that her social message will gain credibility more immediately from the *witness of actions* than as a result of its internal logic and consistency. This awareness is also a source of her preferential option for the poor, which is never exclusive or discriminatory towards other groups.

This option is not limited to material poverty, since it is well known that there are many other forms of poverty, especially in modern society—not only economic but cultural and spiritual poverty as well. The Church's love for the poor, which is essential for her and a part of her constant tradition, impels her to give attention to a world in which poverty is threatening to assume massive proportions in spite of technological and economic progress. In the countries of the West, different forms of poverty are being experienced by groups which live on the margins of society, by the elderly and the sick, by the victims of consumerism, and even more immediately by so many refugees and migrants. In the developing countries, tragic crises loom on the horizon unless internationally coordinated measures are taken before it is too late. [1]

The Gift of Grace

Love for others, and in the first place love for the poor, in whom the Church sees Christ himself, is made concrete in the *promotion of justice*. Justice will never be fully attained unless people see in the poor person, who is asking for help in order to survive, not an annoyance or a burden, but an opportunity for showing kindness and a chance for greater enrichment. Only such an awareness can give the courage needed to face the risk and the change involved in every authentic attempt to come to the aid of another. It is not merely a matter of "giving from one's surplus," but of helping entire peoples which are presently excluded or marginalized to enter into the sphere of economic and human development. For this to happen, it is not enough to draw on the surplus goods which in fact our world abundantly produces; it requires above all a change of lifestyles, of models of production and consumption, and of the established structures of power which today govern societies. [2]

Therefore, in order that the demands of justice be met, and attempts to achieve this goal may succeed, what is needed is *the gift of grace, a gift* which comes from God. Grace, in cooperation with human freedom, constitutes that mysterious presence of God in history which is Providence. [3]

PROGRESS THAT IS WORTHY OF MAN

The man of today seems ever to be under threat from what he produces, that is to say from the result of the work of his hands and, even more so, of the work of his intellect and the tendencies of his will. All too soon, and often in an unforeseeable way, what this manifold activity of man yields is not only subjected to "alienation," in the sense that it is simply taken away from the person who produces it, but rather it turns against man himself, at least in part, through the indirect consequences of its effects returning on himself. It is or can be directed against him. This seems to make up the main chapter of the drama of present-day human existence in its broadest and universal dimension.

Man therefore lives increasingly in fear. He is afraid that what he produces—not all of it, of course, or even most of it, but part of it and precisely that part that contains a special share of his genius and initiative—can radically turn against himself; he is afraid that it can become the means and instrument for an unimaginable self-destruction, compared with which all the cataclysms and catastrophes of history known to us seem to fade away. This gives rise to a question: Why is it that the power given to man from the beginning by which he was to subdue the earth (cf. Genesis 1:28) turns against himself, producing an understandable state of disquiet, of conscious or unconscious fear and of menace, which in various ways is being communicated to the whole of the present-day human family and is manifesting itself under various aspects?

This state of menace for man from what he produces shows itself in various directions and various degrees of intensity. We seem to be increasingly aware of the fact that the exploitation of the earth, the planet on which we are living, demands rational and honest planning. . . . Man often seems to see no other meaning in his natural environment than what serves for immediate use and consumption. Yet it was the Creator's will that man should communicate with nature as an intelligent and noble "master" and "guardian," and not as a heedless "exploiter" and "destroyer."

The Goal of Human Development

The development of technology and the development of contemporary civilization, which is marked by the ascendancy of technology, demand a proportional development of morals and ethics. For the present, this last development seems unfortunately to be always left behind. Accordingly, in spite of the marvel of this progress, in which it is difficult not to see also authentic signs of man's greatness, signs that in their creative seeds were revealed to us in the pages of the book of Genesis, as early as where it describes man's creation (cf. Genesis 1-2), this progress cannot fail to give rise to disquiet on many counts.

The first reason for disquiet concerns the essential and fundamental question: Does this progress, which has man for its author and promoter, make human life on earth "more human" in every aspect of that life? Does it make it more "worthy of man"? There can be no doubt that in various aspects it does. But the question keeps coming back with regard to what is most essential—whether in the context of this progress man, as man, is becoming truly better, that is to say more mature spiritually, more aware of the dignity of his humanity, more responsible, more open to others, especially the neediest and the weakest, and readier to give and to aid all. [4] ∾

THE "TRUE GOOD" OF THE HUMAN RACE

There is a better understanding today that the *mere accumulation* of goods and services, even for the benefit of the majority, is not enough for the realization of human happiness. Nor, in consequence, does the availability of the many *real benefits* provided in recent times by science and technology, including the computer sciences, bring freedom from every form of slavery. On the contrary, the experience of recent years shows that unless all the considerable body of resources and potential at man's disposal is guided by *a moral understanding* and by an orientation towards the true good of the human race, it easily turns against man to oppress him.

A *disconcerting conclusion* about the most recent period should serve to enlighten us: side-by-side with the miseries of underdevelopment, themselves unacceptable, we find ourselves up against a form of *superdevelopment,* equally inadmissible, because like the former it is contrary to what is good and to true happiness. This superdevelopment, which consists in an *excessive* availability of every kind of material goods for the benefit of certain social groups, easily makes people slaves of "possession" and of immediate gratification, with no other horizon than the multiplication or continual replacement of the things already owned with others still better. This is the so-called civilization of "consumption" or "consumerism," which involves so much "throwing-away" and "waste." An object already owned but now superseded by something better is discarded, with no thought of its possible lasting value in itself, nor of some other human being who is poorer.

All of us experience firsthand the sad effects of this blind submission to pure consumerism: in the first place a crass materialism, and at the same time a *radical dissatisfaction*, because one quickly learns—unless one is shielded from the flood of publicity and the ceaseless and tempting offers of products—that the more one possesses the more one wants, while deeper aspirations remain unsatisfied and perhaps even stifled. [5]

Image and Likeness

In trying to achieve true development we must never lose sight of that *dimension* which is in the *specific nature* of man, who has been created by God in his image and likeness (cf. Genesis 1:26). It is a bodily and a spiritual nature, symbolized in the second creation account by the two elements: the *earth*, from which

God forms man's body, and the *breath of life* which he breathes into man's nostrils (cf. Genesis 2:7).

Thus man comes to have a certain affinity with other creatures: he is called to use them, and to be involved with them. As the Genesis account says (cf. Genesis 2:15), he is placed in the garden with the duty of cultivating and watching over it, being superior to the other creatures placed by God under his dominion (cf. Genesis 1:25-26). But at the same time man must remain subject to the will of God, who imposes limits upon his use and dominion over things (cf. Genesis 2:16-17), just as he promises him immortality (cf. Genesis 2:9; Wisdom 2:23). Thus man, being the image of God, has a true affinity with him too.

On the basis of this teaching, development cannot consist only in the use, dominion over and *indiscriminate* possession of created things and the products of human industry, but rather in subordinating the possession, dominion and use to man's divine likeness and to his vocation to immortality. This is the *transcendent reality* of the human being, a reality which is seen to be shared from the beginning by a couple, a man and a woman (cf. Genesis 1:27), and is therefore fundamentally social. [6]

Inheriting Immortality

Here the perspectives widen. The dream of "unlimited progress" reappears, radically transformed by the *new outlook* created by Christian faith, assuring us that progress is possible only because God the Father has decided from the beginning to make man a sharer of his glory in Jesus Christ risen from the dead, in whom "we have redemption through his blood . . . the forgiveness of our trespasses" (Ephesians 1:7). In him God wished to conquer sin and make it serve our greater good, which infinitely surpasses what progress could achieve.

We can say therefore—as we struggle amidst the obscurities and deficiencies of *underdevelopment and superdevelopment*—that one day this corruptible body will put on incorruptibility, this mortal body immortality (cf. 1 Corinthians 15:54), when the Lord "delivers the kingdom to God the Father" (15:24) and all the works and actions that are worthy of man will be redeemed. [7]

The Way to Freedom

Development which is merely economic is incapable of setting man free; on the contrary, it will end by enslaving him further. Development that does not include the *cultural, transcendent and religious dimensions* of man and society, to the extent that it does not recognize the existence of such dimensions and does not endeavor to direct its goals and priorities toward the same, is *even less* conducive to authentic liberation. Human beings are totally free only when they are completely *themselves*, in the fullness of their rights and duties. The same can be said about society as a whole.

The principal obstacle to be overcome on the way to authentic liberation is *sin* and the *structures* produced by sin as it multiplies and spreads (*Reconciliato et Paenitentia*, 16).

The freedom with which Christ has set us free (cf. Galatians 5:1) encourages us to become the *servants* of all. Thus the process of *development* and *liberation* takes concrete shape in the exercise of *solidarity*, that is to say in the love and service of neighbor, especially of the poorest: "For where truth and love are missing, the process of liberation results in the death of a freedom which will have lost all support" (Congregation for the Doctrine of the Faith, *Libertatis Conscientia*, 24). [8]

Securing Peaceful Development

In the context of the *sad experiences* of recent years and of the *mainly negative picture* of the present moment, the Church must strongly affirm the *possibility* of overcoming the obstacles which, by excess or by defect, stand in the way of development. And she must affirm her confidence in a *true liberation*. Ultimately, this confidence and this possibility are based on the *Church's awareness* of the divine promise guaranteeing that our present history does not remain closed in upon itself but is open to the kingdom of God.

The Church has *confidence also in man*, though she knows the evil of which he is capable. For she well knows that—in spite of the heritage of sin, and the sin which each one is capable of committing—there exist in the human person sufficient qualities and energies, a fundamental "goodness" (cf. Genesis 1:31), because he is the image of the Creator, placed under the redemptive influence of Christ, who "united himself in some fashion with every man" (Vatican II, *Pastoral Constitution on the Church in the Modern World*, 22), and because the efficacious action of the Holy Spirit "fills the earth" (Wisdom 1:7).

There is no justification then for despair or pessimism or inertia. Though it be with sorrow, it must be said that just as one may sin through selfishness and the desire for excessive profit and power, *one may also be found wanting* with regard to the urgent needs of multitudes of human beings submerged in conditions of underdevelopment, through *fear, indecision* and, basically, through *cowardice*. We are *all* called, indeed *obliged*, to face the tremendous challenge of the last decade of the second Millennium, also because the present dangers threaten everyone: a world economic crisis, a war without frontiers, without winners or losers. In the face of such a threat, the distinction between rich individuals and countries and poor individuals and countries *will have little value*, except that a greater responsibility rests on those who have more and can do more.

This is not however *the sole motive or even the most important one*. At stake is the *dignity of the human person*, whose *defense* and *promotion* have been entrusted to us by the Creator, and to whom the men and women at every moment of history are strictly and responsibly *in debt*. As many people are already more or less clearly aware, the present situation *does not seem to correspond to* this dignity. *Every individual* is called upon to play his or her part in this *peaceful* campaign, a campaign to be conducted by *peaceful* means, in order to secure *development in peace*, in order to safeguard nature itself and the world about us. The Church too feels profoundly involved in this enterprise, and she hopes for its ultimate success. [9] ∾

Welcoming the New Millennium

A New Springtime for the Gospel

As the third millennium of the redemption draws near, God is preparing a great springtime for Christianity, and we can already see its first signs. In fact, both in the non-Christian world and in the traditionally Christian world, people are gradually drawing closer to gospel ideals and values, a development which the Church seeks to encourage. Today in fact there is a new consensus among peoples about these values: the rejection of violence and war; respect for the human person and for human rights; the desire for freedom, justice and brotherhood; the surmounting of different forms of racism and nationalism; the affirmation of the dignity and role of women.

Christian hope sustains us in committing ourselves fully to the new evangelization and to the worldwide mission, and leads us to pray as Jesus taught us: "Thy kingdom come. Thy will be done, on earth as it is in heaven" (Matthew 6:10).

The number of those awaiting Christ is still immense: the human and cultural groups not yet reached by the gospel, or for whom the Church is scarcely present, are so widespread as to require the uniting of all the Church's resources. As she prepares to celebrate the Jubilee of the Year 2000, the whole Church is even more committed to a new missionary advent. We must increase our apostolic zeal to pass on to others the light and joy of the faith, and to this high ideal the whole People of God must be educated. [1]

THE JOY OF THE GREAT JUBILEE

The term "Jubilee" speaks of joy—not just an inner joy but a jubilation which is manifested outwardly, for the coming of God is also an outward, visible, audible and tangible event, as St. John makes clear (cf. 1 John 1:1). It is thus appropriate that every sign of joy at this coming should have its own outward expression. This will demonstrate that the Church rejoices in salvation. She invites everyone to rejoice, and she tries to create conditions to ensure that the power of salvation may be shared by all. Hence the Year 2000 will be celebrated as the Great Jubilee.

With regard to its content, this Great Jubilee will be, in a certain sense, like any other. But at the same time it will be different, greater than any other. For the Church respects the measurements of time: hours, days, years, centuries. She thus goes forward with every individual, helping everyone to realize how *each of these measurements of time is imbued with the presence of God* and with his saving activity. In this spirit the Church rejoices, gives thanks and asks forgiveness, presenting her petitions to the Lord of history and of human consciences. [2]

In the Church's history every jubilee is prepared for by Divine Providence. This is true also of the Great Jubilee of the Year 2000. With this conviction, we look today with a sense of gratitude and yet with a sense of responsibility at all that has happened in human history since the birth of Christ, particularly the events which have occurred between the years 1000 and 2000. But in a very particular way, we look with the eyes of faith to our own century, searching out whatever bears witness not only to man's history but also to God's intervention in human affairs. [3]

The Gift of Vatican II

From this point of view we can affirm that *the Second Vatican Council was a providential event, whereby the Church began the more immediate preparation* for the Jubilee of the Second Millennium. It was a Council similar to earlier ones, yet very different; it was a Council *focused on the mystery of Christ and his Church and at the same time open to the world.* This openness was an evangelical response to recent changes in the world, including the profoundly disturbing experiences of the twentieth century, a century scarred by the First and Second World Wars, by the experience of concentration camps and by horrendous massacres. All these events demonstrate most vividly that the world needs purification; it needs to be converted.

The Second Vatican Council is often considered as the beginning of a new era in the life of the Church. This is true, but at the same time it is difficult to overlook the fact that the *Council drew much from the experiences and reflections of the immediate past,* especially from the intellectual legacy left by Pius XII. In the history of the Church, the "old" and the "new" are always closely interwoven. The "new" grows out of the "old," and the "old" finds a fuller expression in the "new." Thus it was for the Second Vatican Council and for the activity of the popes connected with the Council, starting with John XXIII, continuing with Paul VI and John Paul I, up to the present Pope.

What these popes have accomplished during and since the Council, in their Magisterium no less than in their pastoral activity, has certainly made a significant contribution to the *preparation of that new springtime of Christian life* which will be revealed by the Great Jubilee, if Christians are docile to the action of the Holy Spirit. [4]

Founded on the Gospel

The Council, while not imitating the sternness of John the Baptist who called for repentance and conversion on the banks of the Jordan (cf. Luke 3:1-7), did show something of the Prophet of old, pointing out with fresh vigor to the men and women of today that Jesus Christ is the "Lamb of God who takes away the sin of the world" (John 1:29), the Redeemer of humanity and the Lord of history. During the Council, precisely out of a desire to be fully faithful to her Master, the Church questioned herself about her own identity, and discovered anew the depth of her mystery as the Body and the Bride of Christ. Humbly heeding the word of God, she reaffirmed the universal call to holiness; she made provision for the reform of the liturgy, the "origin and summit" of her life; she gave impetus to the renewal of many aspects of her life at the universal level and in the local Churches; she strove to promote the various Christian vocations, from those of the laity to those of religious, from the ministry of deacons to that of priests and bishops; and in a particular way she rediscovered episcopal collegiality, that privileged expression of the pastoral service carried out by the bishops in communion with the Successor of Peter.

On the basis of this profound renewal, the Council opened itself to Christians of other denominations, to the followers of other religions and to all the people of our time. No Council had ever spoken so clearly about Christian unity, about dialogue with non-Christian religions, about the specific meaning of the Old Covenant and of Israel, about the dignity of each person's conscience, about the principle of religious liberty, about the different cultural traditions within which the Church carries out her missionary mandate, and about the means of social communication. [5]

Proclaiming a New Era

The Council's enormously rich body of teaching and *the striking new tone* in the way it presented this content constitute as it were a proclamation of new times. The Council Fathers spoke in the language of the gospel, the language of the Sermon on the Mount and the beatitudes. In the Council's message God is presented *in his absolute lordship over all things, but also as the One who ensures the authentic autonomy of earthly realities.*

The best preparation for the new millennium, therefore, can only be expressed in a renewed commitment *to apply,* as faithfully as possible, *the teachings of Vatican II to the life of every individual and of the whole Church.* It was with the Second Vatican Council that, in the broadest sense of the term, the immediate preparations for the Great Jubilee of the Year 2000 were really begun. If we look for an analogy in the liturgy, it could be said that the yearly *Advent liturgy* is the season nearest to the spirit of the Council. For Advent prepares us to meet the One who was, who is and who is to come (cf. Revelation 4:8). [6]

LET US HASTEN TO THE JUBILEE FEAST

The journey of believers towards the Third Millennium is in no way weighed down by the weariness which the burden of two thousand years of history could bring with it. Rather, Christians feel invigorated, in the knowledge that they bring to the world the true light, Christ the Lord. Proclaiming Jesus of Nazareth, true God and perfect Man, the Church opens to all people the prospect of being "divinized" and thus of becoming more human (Vatican II, *Pastoral Constitution on the Church in the Modern World*, 41). This is the one path which can lead the world to discover its lofty calling and to achieve it fully in the salvation wrought by God. [7]

The particular churches during these years of immediate preparation for the Jubilee are getting ready, through prayer, catechesis and pastoral action of different kinds, for this celebration which is leading the whole Church into a new time of grace and mission. The approach of the Jubilee is also evoking growing interest among those who are searching for a favorable sign to help them discern the traces of God's presence in our time.

The years of preparation for the Jubilee have been placed under the sign of the Most Holy Trinity: through Christ—in the Holy Spirit—to God the Father. In the mystery of the Trinity, the journey of faith has its origin and its final goal, when at last our eyes will contemplate the face of God for ever. In celebrating the Incarnation, we fix our gaze upon the mystery of the Trinity. Jesus of Nazareth, who reveals the Father, has fulfilled the desire hidden in every human heart to know God. What creation preserved as a seal etched in it by the creative hand of God and what the ancient Prophets had announced as a promise is disclosed in the revelation of Christ (Vatican II, *Dogmatic Constitution on Divine Revelation*, 2,4).

A Hymn of Praise

Jesus reveals the face of God the Father "compassionate and merciful" (James 5:11), and with the sending of the Holy Spirit he makes known the mystery of love which is the Trinity. It is the Spirit of Christ who is at work in the Church and in history: we must listen to him in order to recognize the signs of the new times and to make the expectation of the glorified Lord's return ever more vibrant in the hearts of the faithful. The Holy Year must therefore be one unceasing hymn of praise to the Trinity, the Most High God.

At this point, the poetic words of St. Gregory of Nazianzus, the Theologian, come to our aid:

Glory to God the Father and to the Son, King of the universe. Glory to the Spirit, worthy of praise and all holy. The Trinity is one God who created and filled all things: the heavens with heavenly beings, the earth with creatures of earth, the sea, the rivers and springs with creatures of the waters, giving life to all things by his Spirit, that all creatures might sing the praises of their wise Creator, who alone gives life and sustains all life in being. Above all others, let the creature who reasons celebrate him always as the great King and good Father. (*Poemi dogmatici*, 31) [8]

In Full Communion

May this hymn to the Trinity for the Incarnation of the Son rise with one voice from all who have been baptized and share the same faith in the Lord Jesus. May the ecumenical character of the Jubilee be a concrete sign of the journey which, especially in recent decades, the faithful of the different Churches and Ecclesial communities have been making. It is only by listening to the Spirit that we shall be able to show forth visibly in full communion the grace of divine adoption which springs from Baptism: all of us children of the one Father.

The challenging call of the Apostle rings out again for us today: "There is one body and one Spirit, just as you were called to the one hope that belongs to your call, one Lord, one faith, one baptism, one God and Father of us all, who is above all and through all and in all" (Ephesians 4:4-6). To use the words of St. Irenaeus: after receiving the Word of God as rain falling from heaven we cannot allow ourselves to present to the world an image of dry earth; nor can we ever claim to be one bread if we prevent the scattered flour from becoming one through the action of the water which has been poured on us (*Contro le eresie*, III).

Every Jubilee Year is like an invitation to a wedding feast. From the different Churches and Ecclesial communities throughout the world, let us all hasten to the feast now being prepared; let us bring with us everything that already unites us and, by fixing our gaze on Christ alone, let us grow in the unity which is the fruit of the Spirit. The present task of the Bishop of Rome, as the Successor of Peter, is to make the invitation to the Jubilee celebration all the more insistent, in order that the two thousandth anniversary of the central mystery of the Christian faith may be experienced as a journey of reconciliation and a sign of true hope for all who look to Christ and to his Church, the sacrament "of intimate union with God and the unity of the entire human race" (Vatican II, *Dogmatic Constitution on the Church*, 1). [9]

Endnotes

Chapter Two: Forgiveness, Reconciliation, Mercy

1. Encyclical Letter *Dives in Misericordia* (The Mercy of God), 14

2. Apostolic Exhortation *Reconciliatio et Paenitentia* (Reconciliation and Penance), 10

3. *Dives in Misericordia*, 5

4. *Ibid.*, 6

5. Encyclical Letter *Redemptor Hominis* (The Redeemer of Man), 9

Chapter Three: Prayer and the Eucharist

1. Encyclical Letter *Dominum et Vivificantem* (The Holy Spirit in the Life of the Church and the World), 65

2. Apostolic Exhortation *Familiaris Consortio* (The Role of the Christian Family in the Modern World), 59

3. *Ibid.*, 60

4. Apostolic Letter *Dies Domini* (On Keeping the Lord's Day Holy), 15

5. *Ibid.*, 31

6. Letter of Pope John Paul II to all the Bishops of the Church, *Dominicae Cenae* (On the Mystery and Worship of the Eucharist), 5

7. *Ibid.*, 6

8. *Ibid.*, 7

9. Encyclical Letter *Redemptor Hominis* (The Redeemer of Man), 20

Chapter Four: Marriage and Family

1. *Letter to Families*, 18

2. Address at Williams-Brice Stadium, Columbia, South Carolina, September 11, 1987. Reprinted from L'Osservatore Romano English edition.

3. Apostolic Exhortation *Familiaris Consortio* (The Role of the Christian Family in the Modern World), 21

Chapter Five: To the Youth of the World

1. Speech delivered to young people at Kiel Center, St. Louis, Missouri, January 26, 1999. Reprinted from L'Osservatore Romano English edition.

2. Speech delivered at Youth Forum Mass, World Youth Day, Denver, Colorado, August 14, 1993. Reprinted from L'Osservatore Romano English edition.

3. Apostolic Letter of Pope John Paul II to the Youth of the World, 9

Chapter Six: The Call to Unity

1. Encyclical Letter *Ut Unum Sint* (That They May Be One), 1

2. *Ibid.*, 3

3. *Ibid.*, 6

4. *Ibid.*, 21

5. *Ibid.*, 102

6. Encyclical Letter *Redemptor Hominis* (The Redeemer of Man), 6

7. General Audience, July 12, 1999. Reprinted from L'Osservatore Romano English edition.

8. Encyclical Letter *Ut Unum Sint* (That They May Be One), 22

9. *Ibid.*, 26

10. *Ibid.*, 27

Chapter Seven: Made in the Image of God

1. Encyclical Letter *Redemptor Hominis* (The Redeemer of Man), 10

2. Encyclical Letter *Evangelium Vitae* (The Gospel of Life), 39

3. *Ibid.*, 44

4. *Ibid.*, 80

5. *Ibid.*, 81

6. Encyclical Letter *Laborem Exercens* (On Human Work), 25

7. Apostolic Letter *Salvifici Doloris* (On the Christian Meaning of Human Suffering), 15

8. *Ibid.*, 16

9. *Ibid.*, 18

Chapter Eight: The Mission of the Church

1. Apostolic Exhortation *Christifideles Laici* (Lay Members of Christ's Faithful People), 33

2. *Ibid.*, 34

3. *Ibid.*, 64

4. Encyclical Letter *Redemptor Hominis* (The Redeemer of Man), 11

5. Encyclical Letter *Veritatis Splendor* (The Splendor of Truth), 106

6. *Ibid.*, 107

7. *Ibid.*, 108

8. Encyclical Letter *Redemptoris Missio* (Mission of the Redeemer), 3

9. *Ibid.*, 11

10. *Ibid.*, 42

11. *Ibid.*, 43

Chapter Nine: Love and Justice

1. Encyclical Letter *Centesimus Annus* (On the Hundredth Anniversary of *Rerum Novarum*), 57

2. *Ibid.*, 58

3. *Ibid.*, 59

4. Encyclical Letter *Redemptor Hominis* (The Redeemer of Man), 15

5. Encyclical Letter *Sollicitudo Rei Socialis* (On Social Concern), 28

6. *Ibid.*, 29

7. *Ibid.*, 31

8. *Ibid.*, 46

9. *Ibid.*, 47

Chapter Ten: Welcoming the New Millennium

1. Encyclical Letter *Redemptoris Missio* (Mission of the Redeemer), 86

2. Apostolic Letter *Tertio Millennio Adveniente* (The Coming of the Third Millennium), 16

3. *Ibid.*, 17

4. *Ibid.*, 18

5. *Ibid.*, 19

6. *Ibid.*, 20

7. Jubilee Bull *Incarnationis Mysterium*, 2

8. *Ibid.*, 3

9. *Ibid.*, 4